Recipes: The Cookin

D0102553

Contents

Foods of the World

TIME-LIFE BOOKS, ALEXANDRIA, VIRGINIA

Hors d'Oeuvre and Dim Sum

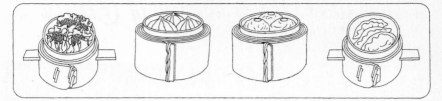

Yu-cha-hün-tün

油炸餛飩

DEEP-FRIED WONTON FILLED WITH PORK AND SHRIMP

To make about 4 dozen *wontons*

One recipe *wonton* wrappers, prepared
  according to the recipe opposite,
  or ½ pound ready-made *wonton*
  wrappers, or 1 pound ready-made
  egg-roll wrappers

THE FILLING
1 pound raw shrimp in their shells
2 tablespoons peanut oil, or flavorless
  vegetable oil
½ pound lean boneless pork, freshly
  ground
2 tablespoons soy sauce

1 tablespoon Chinese rice wine, or
  pale dry sherry
1 teaspoon salt
6 peeled and washed fresh water-
  chestnuts, or drained canned water
  chestnuts, finely chopped
1 scallion, including the green top,
  finely chopped
1 teaspoon cornstarch dissolved in 1
  tablespoon cold chicken stock,
  fresh or canned, or cold water

3 cups peanut oil, or flavorless
  vegetable oil

PREPARE AHEAD: 1. Shell the shrimp. With a small, sharp knife, make an incision down their backs and lift out the black or white intestinal vein with the point of the knife. Chop the shrimp fine.

2. To prepare the filling: Set a 12-inch wok or 10-inch skillet over high heat for 30 seconds. Pour in the 2 tablespoons of oil, swirl it about in the pan and heat for another 30 seconds, turning the heat down if the oil begins to smoke. Add the pork and stir-fry for 1 minute, or until the meat loses its reddish color. Add the shrimp, soy sauce, wine, salt, water chestnuts and scallions, and stir-fry for another minute, or until the shrimp turn pink. Give the cornstarch mixture a stir to recombine it and pour it into the pan. Stir constantly until the liquid thickens, then transfer the contents of the pan to a bowl and cool to room temperature.

3. Cut homemade *wonton* wrappers or ready-made egg-roll wrappers into 3½-inch squares. Ready-made *wonton* wrappers are already cut.

4. To assemble the *wontons:* Place 1½ teaspoons of the filling in the center of each *wonton* wrapper. With a finger dipped in water, moisten the edges of the wrapper. Then bring one corner up over the filling to the op-

posite corner, but fold the wrapper at an angle so that two overlapping triangles are formed, with their points side by side and about ½ inch apart. Pull the two bottom corners of the folded triangle forward and below the folded edge so that they meet one another and slightly overlap, to create a kind of frame around the mound of the filling. Moisten one end with a finger dipped in water and pinch the two ends firmly together. As each *wonton* is finished, place it on a plate and cover it with a dry towel. If the *wontons* must wait longer than 30 minutes before cooking, cover them with plastic wrap and refrigerate.

TO COOK: Set a 12-inch wok or 10-inch skillet over high heat and pour 3 cups of oil into it. Heat the oil until a haze forms above it or it registers 375° on a deep-frying thermometer. Deep-fry the *wontons*, 8 or 10 at a time, for 2 minutes, or until they are crisp and golden. Transfer them to paper towels to drain while you fry the rest. Serve attractively arranged on a heated platter. Fried *wontons* can be kept warm for an hour or so in a 250° oven, or reheated for 5 minutes in a 450° oven.

Hün-t'un-pi   餛飩皮
WONTON WRAPPERS

To make about 4 dozen *wonton*
   wrappers
4 cups sifted all-purpose flour
1 teaspoon salt
2 eggs, lightly beaten
1 cup cold water

1. Sift the flour and salt into a bowl, make a well in the center and pour into it the eggs and cold water. With your fingers or a spoon, mix the flour and liquid ingredients together until they can be gathered into a soft ball. Knead the dough in the bowl for 4 to 5 minutes, or until it is smooth but still soft. Do not overknead or the dough will become stiff.

2. Divide the dough into 4 equal-sized balls. On a lightly floured surface, roll one ball at a time into a 14-inch square about 1/16 inch thick. For soup *wonton (page 23)* or deep-fried *wonton (opposite)*, cut the dough into 3½-inch squares with a sharp knife or pastry wheel. For steamed pork dumplings *(page 14)*, use a 3-inch cookie cutter or the rim of a glass to cut the dough into rounds. If the wrappers must rest for any length of time, cover them with a lightly dampened towel. If you wish to freeze them, wrap them securely in foil or plastic wrap.

Ch'un-chüan

春捲

EGG ROLLS WITH SHRIMP AND PORK

To make 16 egg rolls

THE FILLING

½ pound fresh bean sprouts or
   substitute a 1-pound can of bean
   sprouts
½ pound raw shrimp in their shells
3 tablespoons oil
½ pound lean boneless pork, finely
   ground
4 cups finely chopped celery
2 to 3 medium fresh mushrooms, cut
   in ¼-inch slices (about ½ cup)
1 tablespoon soy sauce
1 tablespoon Chinese rice wine, or
   pale dry sherry

2 teaspoons salt
½ teaspoon sugar
1 tablespoon cornstarch dissolved in
   2 tablespoons cold chicken stock,
   fresh or canned, or cold water

THE WRAPPERS

2 cups flour
½ teaspoon salt
¾ cup cold water
1 egg, lightly beaten
Note: 1 pound ready-made egg-roll
   wrappers may be substituted for
   these homemade wrappers

3 cups peanut oil, or flavorless
   vegetable oil

PREPARE AHEAD: 1. Rinse the fresh bean sprouts in a pot of cold water and discard any husks that float to the surface. Drain and pat them dry with paper towels. To crisp canned bean sprouts, rinse them under running water and refrigerate them in a bowl of cold water for at least 2 hours. Drain and pat them dry before using.

2. Shell the shrimp. With a small, sharp knife, devein them by making a shallow incision down their backs and lifting out the black or white intestinal vein with the point of the knife. Using a cleaver or large knife, cut the shrimp into fine dice.

3. TO MAKE THE FILLING: Set a 12-inch wok or 10-inch skillet over high heat for 30 seconds. Pour in 1 tablespoon of oil, swirl it about in the pan and heat for another 30 seconds, turning the heat down to moderate if the oil begins to smoke. Add the pork and stir-fry for 2 minutes, or until it loses its reddish color. Then add the wine, soy sauce, sugar, shrimp and mushrooms, and stir-fry for another minute, or until the shrimp turn pink. Transfer the entire contents of the pan to a bowl and set aside.

Pour the remaining 2 tablespoons of oil into the same wok or skillet, swirl it about in the pan and heat for 30 seconds, turning the heat down to moderate if the oil begins to smoke. Add the celery and stir-fry for 5 minutes, then add the salt and bean sprouts, and mix thoroughly together. Return the pork and shrimp mixture to the pan, and stir until all the ingredients are well combined. Cook over moderate heat, stirring constantly, until the liquid starts to boil.

There should be about 2 or 3 tablespoons of liquid remaining in the pan. If there is more, spoon it out and discard it. Give the cornstarch mixture a quick stir to recombine it, and add it, stirring until the cooking liquids have thickened slightly and coated the mixture with a light glaze. Transfer the entire contents of the pan to a bowl and cool to room temperature before using.

4. TO MAKE THE WRAPPERS: Sift the flour and salt into a large mixing bowl. With a large spoon or your hands, gradually combine the flour and salt with the water, mixing until a stiff dough is formed. Knead the dough in the bowl for 5 minutes, or until it is smooth, then cover the bowl with a dampened cloth and let it rest for 30 minutes. Turn the dough out on a lightly floured surface and firmly roll it out until it is no more than 1/16 inch thick. With a cookie cutter, pastry wheel or sharp knife, cut the dough into 7-inch squares. When you have finished, there should be 16 squares.

TO ASSEMBLE: For each egg roll, shape about 1/4 cup of filling with your hands into a cylinder about 4 inches long and an inch in diameter, and place it diagonally across the center of a wrapper. Lift the lower triangular flap over the filling and tuck the point under it, leaving the upper point of the wrapper exposed. Bring each of the two small end flaps, one at a time, up to the top of the enclosed filling and press the points firmly down. Brush the upper and exposed triangle of dough with lightly beaten egg and then roll the wrapper into a neat package. The beaten egg will seal the edges and keep the wrapper intact.

Place the filled egg rolls on a plate and cover them with a dry kitchen towel. If they must wait longer than about 30 minutes before being fried, cover them with plastic wrap and place them in the refrigerator.

TO COOK: Set a 12-inch wok or heavy deep-fryer over high heat, add 3 cups of oil and heat it until a haze forms above it or it reaches a temperature of 375° on a deep-frying thermometer. Place 5 or 6 egg rolls in the hot oil and deep-fry them for 3 to 4 minutes, or until they have become golden brown and are crisp. Transfer the egg rolls to a double thickness of paper towels and let the oil drain off while you deep-fry another batch of 5 or 6.

Serve the rolls as soon as possible, arranged attractively on a large heated platter. If necessary, the egg rolls can be kept warm for an hour or so in a preheated 250° oven, or they can be reheated for about 10 minutes in a 450° oven.

TO MAKE SPRING ROLLS: Substitute 1 pound fresh, ready-made spring-roll wrappers for the egg-roll wrappers. Prepare the filling according to the recipe already given, then assemble the rolls and deep-fry them as described above.

Because preparing spring-roll wrappers from scratch is so demanding and precise a culinary operation, even the fussiest Chinese cook prefers to use the ready-made variety.

Hsia-jen-tu-ssŭ
蝦仁吐司

DEEP-FRIED SHRIMP TOAST

To make 16 hors d'oeuvre

½ pound fresh shrimp in their shells
4 slices homemade-type white bread
2 tablespoons fresh pork fat
4 peeled fresh water chestnuts or
   rinsed, drained canned water
   chestnuts
1 tablespoon Chinese rice wine, or

pale dry sherry
1 teaspoon salt
1 egg, lightly beaten
2 tablespoons cornstarch
3 cups peanut oil, or flavorless
   vegetable oil
16 leaves of fresh Chinese parsley
   (*cilantro*), or substitute flat-leaf
   Italian parsley

PREPARE AHEAD: 1. Shell the shrimp. With a small, sharp knife, devein them by making a shallow incision down their backs and lifting out the black or white intestinal vein with the point of the knife. With a cleaver or heavy, sharp knife, chop the shrimp until they are reduced to a fine pulp-like mass.

2. With a cleaver or sharp knife, trim the bread slices of their crusts and discard the crusts. Cut the bread into quarters or, diagonally, into triangles.

3. Chop the pork fat and water chestnuts together as fine as possible, and, in a small bowl, combine them with the shrimp. Add the wine, salt, lightly beaten egg and cornstarch, and, with a large spoon or your fingers, mix them together thoroughly until they form a paste.

4. With a knife or spatula, spread an equal amount of the shrimp mixture on the bread squares or triangles, mounding them slightly in the centers. For decoration, gently press a fresh parsley leaf into the center of each mound.

5. Have the above ingredients, the oil, and a large, shallow baking pan lined with a double thickness of paper towels within easy reach.

TO COOK: Preheat the oven to 250°. Pour 3 cups of oil into a 12-inch wok or large deep-fryer and heat the oil until a haze forms above it or it registers 375° on a deep-frying thermometer. Shrimp side down, drop in the bread squares about 6 at a time (the filling will not fall off). Fry for about 1 minute, then gently turn them over in the fat with a large slotted spoon. Fry for 1 minute longer until the bread and shrimp topping are golden brown. Then turn them over again and fry them for another minute. Drain each batch in the lined baking pan and keep them warm in the oven until all the shrimp toast is fried. Serve on a heated platter as an hors d'oeuvre.

Tung-ku-nidng-jou 冬菇釀肉

BRAISED CHINESE MUSHROOMS STUFFED WITH PORK AND WATER CHESTNUTS

20 dried Chinese mushrooms, 1 to 1½ inches in diameter, or substitute fresh mushrooms
1 tablespoon soy sauce
1 tablespoon Chinese rice wine, or pale dry sherry
½ teaspoon sugar
2 teaspoons cornstarch
½ pound boneless pork shoulder, finely ground

4 peeled fresh water chestnuts or drained canned water chestnuts, finely chopped
20 small leaves of Chinese parsley (*cilantro*), or substitute flat-leaf Italian parsley
1 tablespoon peanut oil, or flavorless vegetable oil
2 tablespoons oyster sauce

PREPARE AHEAD: 1. In a small bowl, cover the mushrooms with 2 cups of warm water and let them soak for 30 minutes. Remove them with a slotted spoon. Strain the mushroom water through a fine sieve and save ¼ cup of it. With a cleaver or sharp knife, cut away and discard the tough stems of the mushrooms.

2. Combine in a small bowl the soy sauce, wine, sugar and 1 teaspoon of the cornstarch, and stir to dissolve the cornstarch. Add the ground pork and water chestnuts, and, with your hands or a large spoon, mix them together thoroughly.

3. Sprinkle a little cornstarch on the stem sides of the mushrooms (using about 1 teaspoon in all), then fill them with the pork mixture—dividing the filling equally among them and smoothing it flat with a small knife or your finger. Place a parsley leaf on top of each filled mushroom.

TO COOK: Set a 12-inch heavy skillet over high heat for about 30 seconds. Pour in 1 tablespoon of oil, swirl it around in the pan, then arrange the mushrooms side by side, stuffing side up, in a single layer in the bottom of the pan. Reduce the heat to moderate and let the mushrooms cook for about a minute to brown them lightly. Pour ¼ cup of the reserved mushroom-soaking water into the pan, bring to a boil and cover the pan tightly. Reduce the heat to its lowest point and simmer the mushrooms for 15 minutes. Then stir the oyster sauce into the pan liquid and, with a large spoon or bulb baster, baste each mushroom lightly. Cover the pan for a moment longer, then transfer the mushrooms to a heated platter with a slotted spatula or spoon. Serve hot. Both as an hors d'oeuvre and as part of a Chinese meal *(page 120)*, this will serve 10.

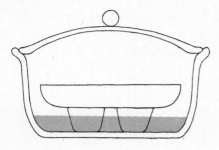

This cutaway view shows the construction of an improvised steamer: A plate is set, two inches above water, on two small, heatproof dishes set right side up in a large, tightly covered roasting pan. There must be enough space around the edge of the plate to allow the steam to rise and circulate freely.

STEAMED BREAD DOUGH

1 package or cake of dry or compressed active yeast	¼ cup lukewarm water
1 tablespoon sugar	1 cup milk, heated to lukewarm
	4 cups sifted all-purpose flour

1. Sprinkle the yeast and sugar into ¼ cup of lukewarm water. Be sure that the water is lukewarm (110° to 115°). If the water is too hot, it will kill the yeast; if it is too cool, the yeast will not be activated. Let the yeast and sugar stand 2 or 3 minutes, then stir together to dissolve them completely. Set the cup in a warm, draft-free place, perhaps a turned-off oven, for 3 to 5 minutes, or until the yeast bubbles up and the mixture almost doubles in volume. If doubling does not take place, discard the mixture and start again with fresh yeast and water.

2. Sift 4 cups of flour into a large mixing bowl. Gradually pour in the yeast mixture and the lukewarm milk, stirring first with a large wooden spoon, and then, when the mixture becomes too difficult to work, with your hands until all the ingredients are well combined and a firm dough is formed.

3. Place the dough on a lightly floured surface and knead it by pressing it down, pushing it forward, then turning it back on itself. Repeat this kneading process for about 5 minutes, sprinkling it with a little flour every now and then to prevent the dough from sticking to the board. Place the dough in a large bowl, cover the bowl with a lightly dampened towel and let it rest in the warm, draft-free place for 1½ to 2 hours, or until the dough doubles in bulk.

4. Punch the dough down with one blow of your fist to reduce it to its original volume. Cover with the towel and let it rise for another 20 to 30 minutes, or until it has again doubled in volume.

5. Turn the dough out on the floured board and knead it as described above for about 5 minutes until it is smooth and elastic. It is now ready to be made into flower rolls (*opposite*) and steamed buns (*pages 10-11*).

Hua-chuän

花捲

STEAMED FLOWER ROLLS

To make 16 rolls

1 recipe steamed bread dough,

prepared according to the
directions opposite

2 tablespoons sesame-seed oil

PREPARE AHEAD: 1. Divide the dough into halves. On a large floured surface, roll out one half of the dough into a rectangle approximately 12 inches long, 8 inches wide and about ¼ inch thick. With a pastry brush, coat the surface of the dough lightly with the sesame-seed oil. Then lift up the long side of the dough and carefully roll it jelly-roll fashion into a long cylinder about 1½ inches in diameter. Roll out the other half of the dough similarly.

2. With a cleaver or sharp knife, slice each cylinder crosswise into rounds ¾ inch thick, and pair the rounds by placing one on top of another, rounded surfaces touching. With a chopstick or the blunt edge of a large knife blade, press down firmly on each pair to make the rounds adhere to each other.

Shape each roll in the following fashion: Holding the ends of the rounds together with your thumbs and forefingers, gently pull the ends away from the center of the bun and then draw the ends backward until they meet. Pinch the ends firmly together to secure them. During this process the oiled layers should separate into flowerlike petals.

3. Place the rolls an inch or two apart on one or two heatproof plates that are ½ inch smaller in diameter than the pot in which you plan to steam them. Cover the rolls with a dry kitchen towel and let them rise for about 30 minutes, or until the dough springs back slowly when lightly poked with a finger.

TO COOK: Pour enough boiling water into the lower part of a steamer to come to within an inch of the cooking rack (or use a steamer substitute as described on page 8). If you have steamer trays, arrange the rolls on two trays—leaving 1-inch spaces between the rolls—and steam them all at one time. Or, if you have a single steamer, or are using the steamer substitute, leave the rolls on the plates on which they rose and place the first plate directly on the rack in the steamer. Bring the water in the steamer to a boil over high heat, cover the pan tightly and steam for 8 minutes. Then transfer the rolls to a heated plate. If you are doing two batches, return the first batch of rolls to the steamer after the second batch is done, piling them on the rolls still in it, and reheat these for 3 or 4 minutes. The extra steaming will not harm the rolls.

Serve the finished rolls on the steaming plate, placed directly on top of a platter, or arranged on a heated platter. Flower rolls are a traditional accompaniment to Szechwan duck *(page 92)* or Mongolian fire pot *(page 28)*.

9

Tou-sha-pao

豆沙乞

STEAMED BUNS WITH DATE FILLING

To make about 2 dozen buns

1 recipe steamed bread dough,
   prepared according to the recipe
   on page 8

THE FILLING
¼ cup lard
1 cup canned red-bean paste
½ pound pitted dates, finely
   chopped
Red food coloring (optional)

These buns are made in the same way as the roast pork steamed buns (*below*), except for the filling, which is prepared in the following fashion: Set a 12-inch wok or 10-inch skillet over moderate heat and add the ¼ cup of lard. When the lard is fully melted, add the canned bean paste and chopped dates, and cook, stirring constantly, for 8 to 10 minutes. Transfer the entire contents of the pan to a bowl and cool thoroughly. With the palms of your hands, roll the filling into balls about 1 inch in diameter. Fill the dough rounds and shape them into buns, as in roast pork buns. Roll the finished buns between the palms of your hands to make them smooth balls. Steam for 10 minutes and serve hot.

    To distinguish the date buns from the pork-filled ones, try following the Chinese custom of dipping the tip of the handle end of a chopstick in red food coloring and stamping a dot on the top of the bun.

Ch'a-shao-pao

义燒乞

STEAMED BUNS WITH ROAST PORK FILLING

To make about 2 dozen buns

1 recipe steamed bread dough,
   prepared according to the recipe
   on page 8

THE FILLING
2 tablespoons peanut oil, or flavorless
   vegetable oil

1 pound roast pork, prepared
   according to the recipe on page
   65, and finely chopped
1 teaspoon sugar
2 tablespoons soy sauce
2 tablespoons cornstarch dissolved in
   3 tablespoons cold chicken stock,
   fresh or canned, or cold water

PREPARE AHEAD: 1. To make the filling: Set a 12-inch wok or 10-inch skillet over high heat for about 30 seconds. Pour in 1 tablespoon of oil, swirl it about in the pan and heat for 30 seconds, turning heat down to moderate if the oil begins to smoke. Add the chopped pork and stir-fry for 1 minute, and then stir in the sugar and soy sauce. Give the cornstarch mixture a quick stir to recombine it and add it to the pan. Cook, stirring constantly, for another 10 seconds, or until the mixture thickens and the pork is covered with a clear glaze. Immediately transfer the entire contents of the pan to a bowl and cool to room temperature.

    2. On a lightly floured surface, form the dough with your hands into a long, sausagelike roll 2 inches in diameter. With a sharp knife, slice the roll into 1-inch rounds. Flatten each round with the palm of your hand,

then with a rolling pin, roll out each round into a disc 4 inches in diameter, turning it counterclockwise as you roll to help keep its circular shape.

3. Place 2 tablespoons of filling in the center of each round. With your fingers, gather the sides of the dough up around filling in loose folds meeting at the top. Then twist the top of the dough firmly closed.

4. Place the buns on 2-inch squares of wax paper, cover them with a dry kitchen towel and let the rolls rise again for 30 minutes, or until the dough springs back slowly when poked gently with a finger.

TO COOK: Pour enough boiling water into the lower part of a steamer to come within an inch of the cooking rack (or use a steamer substitute as described on page 8). If you have steamer trays, arrange the buns an inch apart on two trays and steam them all at one time. In single steamers, place half of the buns on the rack in the steamer, leaving 1-inch spaces between them. Over high heat, bring the water in the steamer to a boil, cover the pan tightly and steam for 10 minutes. Then transfer the buns to a heated plate. If you are doing two batches, return the first batch of buns to the steamer after the second batch is done, piling them on the buns still on the rack. Reheat together for 3 or 4 minutes. Arrange the buns on a heated platter and serve hot.

Chiao-tzŭ and Kuo-tioh 餃子　鍋貼

BOILED OR FRIED PORK DUMPLINGS, NORTHERN STYLE

To make about 4 dozen dumplings

THE DOUGH
2 cups sifted all-purpose flour
¾ cup cold water

THE FILLING
½ pound Chinese cabbage (celery cabbage or *bok choy*)
1 pound lean boneless pork, finely ground
1 teaspoon finely chopped, peeled

fresh ginger root
1 tablespoon Chinese rice wine, or pale dry sherry
1 tablespoon soy sauce
1 teaspoon salt
1 tablespoon sesame-seed oil
2 tablespoons peanut oil, or flavorless vegetable oil
1 cup chicken stock, fresh or canned
¼ cup soy sauce combined with 2 tablespoons white vinegar

PREPARE AHEAD: To make the filling: 1. With a cleaver or heavy, sharp knife, trim the wilted leaves and root ends from the cabbage, and separate the cabbage into stalks. Wash the stalks under cold running water, drain and chop them very fine. Then place the chopped cabbage in a kitchen towel or double layer of cheesecloth and squeeze it firmly to extract as much of its moisture as possible.

2. In a large bowl, combine the ground pork, chopped ginger root, wine, soy sauce, salt and sesame-seed oil, and then add the chopped cabbage. With your hands or a large spoon, mix all the ingredients together until they are thoroughly blended.

Continued on page 14　　11

Making Dumplings

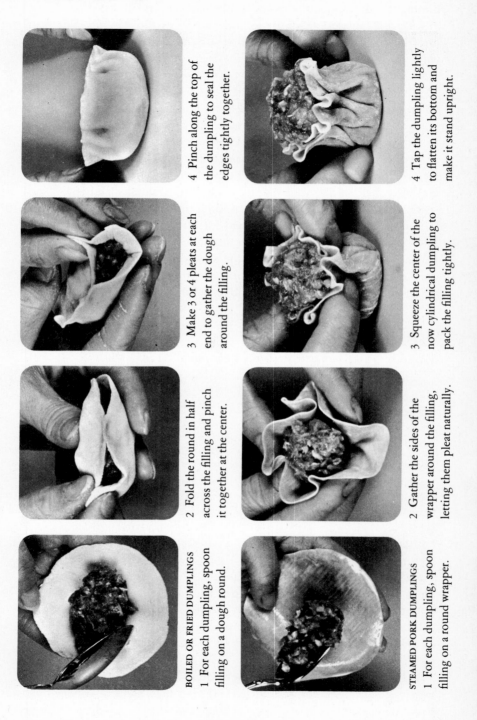

BOILED OR FRIED DUMPLINGS
1 For each dumpling, spoon filling on a dough round.

2 Fold the round in half across the filling and pinch it together at the center.

3 Make 3 or 4 pleats at each end to gather the dough around the filling.

4 Pinch along the top of the dumpling to seal the edges tightly together.

STEAMED PORK DUMPLINGS
1 For each dumpling, spoon filling on a round wrapper.

2 Gather the sides of the wrapper around the filling, letting them pleat naturally.

3 Squeeze the center of the now cylindrical dumpling to pack the filling tightly.

4 Tap the dumpling lightly to flatten its bottom and make it stand upright.

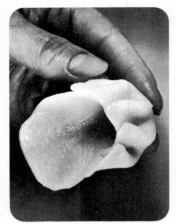

3 Lift up the opposite side with your fingers and gently shape the wrapper into a pouch form.

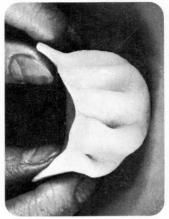

6 Pinch the two ends up slightly to give the finished dumpling the appearance of a Dutch cap.

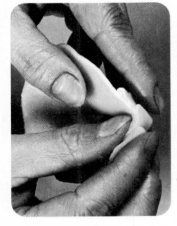

2 Continue making small, even folds along the edge until this side of the wrapper is fully pleated.

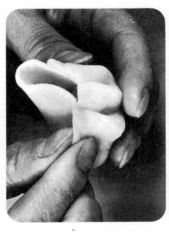

5 Press the pleated and plain sides of the dumpling firmly together to seal the edges tightly.

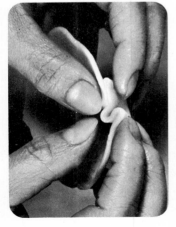

STEAMED SHRIMP DUMPLINGS

1 Begin shaping each oval wrapper by pleating the end of one long side.

4 Fill the pouch with 2 teaspoons of the shrimp mixture, pushing the filling into place with a spatula.

TO MAKE THE DOUGH: 1. Sift the flour into a mixing bowl and, with your hands or a large spoon, gradually combine it with the water, mixing until a stiff dough is formed. Knead the dough in the bowl for 5 minutes, or until it is smooth, then cover the bowl with a dampened cloth and let the dough rest for 30 minutes.

2. Turn the dough out on a lightly floured surface and knead it for another 2 or 3 minutes. Divide the dough into two parts, and, with your hands, firmly shape each piece into a sausagelike cylinder about 12 inches long and 1 inch in diameter.

3. With a cleaver or sharp knife, cut the rolls of dough crosswise into ½-inch slices. Lay the slices on a lightly floured surface and sprinkle their tops with a light dusting of flour. One at a time, press the slices with the palm of your hand to flatten them to about ¼ inch thickness. Then roll each slice with a rolling pin into a 3-inch-round shape about ⅛ inch thick, turning it an inch or so in a clockwise direction as you roll so that the circle keeps its shape. Arrange the rounds side by side on a lightly floured tray or cookie sheet. Cover with a dry kitchen towel.

TO ASSEMBLE: For each dumpling, place 2 teaspoonfuls of the filling in the center of a round of dough and shape the filling into a strip about 1½ inches long. Fold the round in half to make a half-moon shape and pinch the edges together at the center of the arc. With your fingers, make three or four small pleats in one side of the opening at each end of the arc to gather the dough around the filling. Pinch all along the top of the dumpling to seal pleated and smooth edges together. Transfer the finished dumpling to the floured tray or cookie sheet and keep it covered with the dry towel while you proceed with the rest.

TO BOIL: In a 4- to 5-quart pot, bring 2 quarts of water to a bubbling boil. Drop in the dumplings and turn them about in the water once with chopsticks or a large slotted spoon to prevent their sticking together. Cover the pot and cook over high heat only until the water comes to a boil. Immediately pour in 1 cup of cold water, re-cover the pot and bring the water in it to a boil again. Repeat this process twice more, adding 1 cup of cold water each time. Then remove the dumplings from the water with a bamboo strainer or slotted spoon.

Arrange the boiled dumplings on a heated platter and serve them at once. Serve the combined soy sauce and vinegar separately as a dip or sauce for the dumplings.

TO FRY: Set a 12-inch skillet over high heat for 30 seconds. Pour in 2 tablespoons of oil and swirl it about in the pan. Place the dumplings, sides just touching, pleated side up, in the pan. Cook over low heat for 2 minutes, or until the bottoms brown lightly. Add 1 cup of chicken stock, cover the pan tightly and cook over moderate heat for about 10 minutes, or until the liquid has been absorbed. Add the remaining 1 tablespoon of oil and gently swirl it about in the skillet. Let the dumplings fry uncovered for 2 minutes longer. With a spatula or large spoon, gently loosen the dumplings from the bottom of the skillet and transfer them browned side up to a heated platter.

Serve the fried dumplings as soon as they are finished. Accompany them with the soy sauce and vinegar, combined in a small bowl, to be used as a dip or sauce for the dumplings.

Shao-mai

STEAMED PORK DUMPLINGS, CANTONESE STYLE

燒賣

To make about 4 dozen dumplings

Wonton wrappers, prepared according to the recipe on page 3 and cut into 3-inch rounds, or substitute ½ pound ready-made *shao mai* wrappers

THE FILLING
2 stalks celery cabbage
1 pound boneless pork shoulder, finely ground

1 tablespoon Chinese rice wine, or pale dry sherry
1 tablespoon soy sauce
2 teaspoons salt
1 teaspoon sugar
¼ cup finely chopped canned bamboo shoots
1 tablespoon cornstarch

PREPARE AHEAD: 1. With a cleaver or heavy, sharp knife, cut off the root ends and trim any wilted green tops from the cabbage stalks. Wash the stalks under cold running water, then drain them thoroughly and chop them into very fine dice. Place the chopped cabbage in a kitchen towel or double layer of cheesecloth and squeeze it firmly to extract as much of its moisture as possible.

2. In a bowl, combine the pork, wine, soy sauce, salt, sugar and cornstarch, and, with a large spoon, mix them thoroughly together. Stir in the cabbage and bamboo shoots.

3. To fill each dumpling, place a *wonton* or *sao mai* wrapper on the palm of your hand and cup it loosely. Place 1 tablespoonful of the filling in the cup. Then, with your other hand, gather the sides of the wrapper around the filling, letting the wrapper pleat naturally. Squeeze the middle gently to make sure the wrapper fits firmly against the filling and to give the cylinder a faintly wasp-waisted look. Tap the dumpling to flatten its bottom so that it can stand upright.

When all the dumplings are made, place them on a greased heatproof plate ½ inch smaller in diameter than the pot in which you plan to steam them. Cover with plastic wrap and refrigerate until you are ready to steam them—but no longer than 2 to 3 hours.

TO COOK: Pour enough boiling water into the lower part of a steamer to come to within an inch of the cooking rack (or use a steamer substitute as described on page 8). Place the plate of dumplings on the rack. Over high heat, bring the water in the steamer to a rolling boil. Cover the pan tightly and, over high heat, steam for 30 minutes.

If the dumplings must be made in 2 or more batches, keep the finished dumplings warm as you proceed with the rest by covering them with a saucepan lid. Or they may be reheated in the steamer for a minute or so before serving. In any case, during the steaming process, it is wise to keep a kettle of boiling water at hand if the water in the steamer boils away and needs replenishing.

Serve the dumplings on the steamer plate set directly on a platter or, with chopsticks, tongs or a slotted spoon, transfer the finished dumplings to a heated platter.

Fen-kuo 粉果
STEAMED CRABMEAT DUMPLINGS

To make about 4 dozen dumplings

THE FILLING
2 dried Chinese mushrooms, 1 to 1½ inches in diameter
½ pound fresh crabmeat or a 7½-ounce can crabmeat
3 tablespoons peanut oil, or flavorless vegetable oil
1 tablespoon finely chopped, peeled fresh ginger root

¼ teaspoon salt
⅛ teaspoon ground white pepper
¼ teaspoon sugar

THE DOUGH
1½ cups wheat starch
½ cup tapioca flour
1½ cups boiling water
1 tablespoon peanut oil, or flavorless vegetable oil

PREPARE AHEAD: 1. To make the filling: In a small bowl, cover the mushrooms with ½ cup of warm water and let them soak for 30 minutes. Then remove the mushrooms with a slotted spoon and discard the water. With a cleaver or sharp knife, cut away and discard the tough stems of the mushrooms and chop the caps as fine as possible. Set them aside.

2. Pick through the crabmeat, discarding any bits or slivers of cartilage. Shred the meat fine and reserve it with the mushrooms.

3. Place the oil, chopped ginger root, salt, white pepper and sugar within easy reach.

4. Set a 12-inch wok or 10-inch skillet over high heat for about 30 seconds. Pour in 3 tablespoons of oil, swirl it about in the pan and heat for another 30 seconds, reducing the heat to moderate if the oil begins to

smoke. Immediately add the ginger and then the mushrooms and crabmeat, and stir-fry for 2 to 3 minutes. Then stir in the salt, pepper and sugar, stir-fry 30 seconds longer, and transfer the entire contents of the pan to a bowl. Cool to room temperature.

5. TO MAKE THE DOUGH: Sift the combined wheat starch and tapioca flour into a large bowl, make a well in the center and pour into it the 1½ cups of boiling water. With chopsticks or a wooden spoon, gradually mix the flour into the water until a soft dough is formed. Add 1 tablespoon of oil and, with your fingers, knead the dough in the bowl for 3 or 4 minutes, or until smooth. Cover the bowl with a damp towel and let the dough rest for about 20 minutes. Lightly rub a little oil on a marble, metal or wooden surface and place half of the dough on it. With the palms of your hands, roll the dough back and forth, shaping it into a cylinder 12 inches long and about 1 inch in diameter. Roll the second half of the dough into a similar cylinder. Using a cleaver or sharp knife, cut both cylinders crosswise into ½-inch slices and lay the slices flat on the oiled surface 2 or 3 inches apart. Then lightly oil one side of the cleaver or knife blade and, with the palm of your hand, firmly press the blade down on each slice of dough, flattening it into a 2½-inch round. Re-oil the cleaver from time to time as you proceed. Cover the rounds with a dry towel.

TO ASSEMBLE: Place a teaspoonful of the cooled crabmeat filling in the middle of each round of dough. Then fold the edges together to make half-moon-shaped pastries, pressing and pinching the edges to seal them securely. Stand the dumplings upright, pinched edges on top, and push them down gently with your fingers to form bases wide enough for the dumplings to stand upright, unsupported. If they are not to be steamed immediately, cover them with plastic wrap and refrigerate.

TO COOK: Pour enough boiling water into the lower part of a steamer to come to within an inch of the cooking rack (or use a steamer substitute as described on page 8). If you have steamer trays, arrange the dumplings on two trays and steam them all at one time. Or, for single steamers, choose a heatproof plate ½ inch smaller than the diameter of the pot, brush the plate with oil and place half of the dumplings on it. Over high heat, bring the water in the steamer to a boil. Put the plate on the rack, or the trays in place, cover the pan tightly and, over high heat, steam for 5 minutes. If you are doing two batches, return the first batch of dumplings to the steamer after the second batch is done and reheat them together in the steamer for a minute or so before serving. In any case, during the steaming process, it is wise to keep a kettle of boiling water at hand if the water in the steamer boils away and needs replenishing. Serve the dumplings on the steamer plate set directly on a platter, or, with chopsticks, tongs or slotted spoon, transfer them to a heated platter.

Hsia-chiao

蝦餃

STEAMED SHRIMP DUMPLINGS

To make about 4 dozen dumplings

THE FILLING
1 pound fresh shrimp in their shells
2 scallions, white parts only, finely
  chopped
4 water chestnuts, finely chopped

Crabmeat dumpling dough, prepared
  according to the recipe on page 16

1 teaspoon soy sauce
1 teaspoon salt
⅛ teaspoon ground white pepper
1 tablespoon peanut oil, or flavorless
  vegetable oil

PREPARE AHEAD: 1. Shell the shrimp and devein them by making a shallow incision down their backs with a small, sharp knife and lifting out their black or white intestinal veins with the point of the knife. Wash the shrimp under cold running water, pat them dry with paper towels and, with a cleaver or large knife, chop them fine.

2. In a bowl, combine the shrimp, scallions, water chestnuts, soy sauce, salt, pepper and oil, and, with a large spoon, mix together thoroughly. Marinate for at least an hour in the refrigerator.

3. TO MAKE THE DUMPLINGS: Lightly rub a little oil on a marble, metal or wooden surface, and place half of the dough on it. With the palms of your hands, roll the dough back and forth, shaping it into a cylinder 12 inches long and about 1 inch in diameter. Roll the second half of the dough into a similar cylinder. Using a cleaver or sharp knife, cut both cylinders crosswise into ½-inch slices and lay the slices flat on the oiled surface 2 or 3 inches apart. Then lightly oil one side of the cleaver or knife blade and, with the palm of your hand, firmly press the blade down on each slice of dough, flattening it into an oval 3 inches long and 2½ inches wide. Re-oil the cleaver from time to time as you proceed. Cover the ovals with a dry towel. With your thumb and forefinger, form small pleats along one long side of each oval and lift the other side up straight to form a sort of pouch. Fill the pouch with about 2 teaspoons of the filling, and press the pleated and plain edges together firmly to seal it. When all the dumplings are made, place them on a greased heatproof platter and cover them with plastic wrap. Refrigerate them until you are ready to steam them, but no longer than 2 or 3 hours.

TO COOK: Steam the dumplings for 10 minutes as described on page 17 for steamed crabmeat dumplings. Serve them hot.

18

Soups and Fire Pots

T'ang-mien
CHINESE NOODLE SOUP

湯麵

To serve 4 to 6

4 dried Chinese mushrooms, 1 to
 1½ inches in diameter
½ cup cooked chicken, sliced ⅛ inch
 thick and cut into 1-inch squares
½ cup roast pork, prepared
 according to the recipe on page
 65, sliced ⅛ inch thick
½ cup Smithfield ham, sliced ⅛ inch

thick and cut into 1-inch squares
¼ cup thinly sliced canned bamboo
 shoots
½ cup loosely packed watercress
 leaves
½ pound fresh Chinese egg noodles,
 or substitute narrow Italian egg
 noodles such as *tagliarini*
1 teaspoon salt
4 cups chicken stock, fresh or canned

PREPARE AHEAD: 1. In a small bowl, cover the mushrooms with ½ cup of warm water and let them soak for 30 minutes. Discard the water. With a cleaver or sharp knife, cut away and discard the tough stems of the mushrooms, and cut the caps in half.

2. Have the mushrooms, noodles, chicken stock, bamboo shoots, watercress, salt, chicken, pork and ham within easy reach.

TO COOK: In a 3- or 4-quart pot, bring 2 quarts of water to a boil over high heat. Drop in the noodles and boil them vigorously, uncovered, for 2 minutes, stirring occasionally. Drain the noodles through a large sieve and run cold water over them to stop their cooking. Now bring the stock to a boil in the same pot, add the mushrooms, bamboo shoots, watercress, salt and noodles, and reduce the heat to low. Simmer, uncovered, for about 2 minutes. To serve, lift the noodles and vegetables out of the simmering soup with a bamboo strainer or slotted spoon, and transfer them to a large tureen or serving bowl. Arrange the chicken, pork and ham on top of them. Pour in the soup stock down one side of the bowl so as not to disturb the arrangement. Serve at once.

Chi-t'ang
CHICKEN STOCK

雞湯

To make about 3 quarts

A 5-pound stewing chicken (or substitute 5 pounds chicken necks, backs or uncooked bones)

2 slices peeled fresh ginger root, each about 1 inch in diameter and ½ inch thick
1 scallion, including the green top, cut into 1-inch lengths

TO COOK: Place the chicken in a 6-quart heavy pot and pour in enough cold water to cover the chicken (about 4 quarts). Drop in the ginger slices and cut-up scallions. Bring the water to a boil over high heat, skim the surface of any scum or foam that rises to the top, then partially cover the pot. Reduce the heat to low and simmer the chicken for about 2 hours, or until it is tender and almost falling apart. Remove the chicken from the stock and set aside for another use, such as in chicken congee *(below)*. Strain the stock through a fine sieve into a large bowl, cool, then refrigerate. The fat that will congeal on the surface can be removed in large pieces and discarded.

Chi'chu
CHICKEN CONGEE

雞粥

To serve 4 to 6

¼ cup long-grain rice
2 tablespoons glutinous rice
2 quarts fresh or canned chicken stock, or 1 quart chicken broth and 1 quart water combined
1 cup cooked chicken, cut into ½-

inch cubes, prepared according to the recipe for chicken stock above
2 teaspoons salt
½ cup finely shredded preserved kohlrabi
1 cup finely shredded lettuce

PREPARE AHEAD: 1. Combine the long-grain and glutinous rice in a 2-quart saucepan, add enough cold water to cover and stir thoroughly. Pour off the rinse water.

2. Have the rice, stock, chicken, salt, kohlrabi and lettuce handy.

TO COOK: In a 4- to 5-quart heavy saucepan, bring the chicken stock to a boil over high heat. Stir in the rice, partially cover the pan, reduce the heat to low and simmer for 2 hours. Add the salt, then the chicken. Then ladle into individual soup bowls. Serve very hot and garnish the bowls with 1 or 2 tablespoons of shredded kohlrabi and lettuce.

Su-mi-t'ang 粟米湯　蟹肉粟未湯

VELVET CORN SOUP

This is a modernized version of a classic recipe. The original dish was made with field corn (not sweet table corn), available and succulent for only a few days at the height of the summer, and thus considered a great treat. Though corn may not seem a "Chinese vegetable," it was brought to China by Spanish and Portuguese explorers, and has been grown there for more than 400 years.

To serve 4

2 large fresh ears of corn, shucked,
　or substitute an 8¾-ounce can of
　creamed corn
2 egg whites
2 tablespoons milk
3 cups chicken stock, fresh or canned

1 teaspoon salt
1 tablespoon cornstarch dissolved in
　2 tablespoons cold chicken stock,
　fresh or canned, or cold water
A ⅛-inch-thick slice cooked
　Smithfield ham, finely chopped
　(about ¼ cup)

PREPARE AHEAD: 1. With a cleaver or sharp knife, slice the kernels of fresh corn from their cobs into a bowl, making sure not to cut too deeply into the cob or to lose any of the milky corn juices.

2. In a small bowl, beat the egg whites with a fork until frothy. Then beat in the 2 tablespoons of milk.

3. Have the corn, egg white mixture, chicken stock, salt, cornstarch mixture and chopped ham within easy reach.

TO COOK: In a 2-quart saucepan, bring the chicken stock to a boil over high heat. Add the corn and salt, and, stirring constantly, bring to a boil again. Give the cornstarch mixture a quick stir to recombine it and pour it into the soup. Cook, stirring constantly, until the soup has thickened and become clear. Then turn off the heat and immediately pour in the egg white mixture, stirring only once. Quickly pour the hot soup into a tureen or individual bowls and sprinkle with the chopped ham.

VARIATION: Velvet corn soup may be made with crabmeat. Increase the stock to 1 quart and add ½ pound of fresh crabmeat or a 7½-ounce can of crabmeat, carefully picked over, with the corn. Omit the ham.

Yen-wo-t'ang

燕窩湯

BIRD'S NEST SOUP

To serve 6

1 cup loosely packed dried bird's nest
1 whole chicken breast, about ¾
  pound
¼ cup cold water
1 teaspoon cornstarch
1 teaspoon salt

2 egg whites
1 quart chicken stock, fresh or canned
⅛ teaspoon ground white pepper
2 tablespoons cornstarch dissolved in
  3 tablespoons cold chicken stock,
  or cold water
A ⅛-inch-thick slice cooked Smithfield ham, minced

PREPARE AHEAD: 1. Place the bird's nest in a medium-sized bowl, add enough warm water to cover and soak the nest for 3 hours. Then, with a pair of tweezers, carefully remove any protruding feathers. Wash the nest thoroughly under running water. Place the bird's nest in a small saucepan, cover it with cold water and bring to a boil over high heat. Boil it uncovered for 5 minutes, then drain and discard the water.

2. Make chicken velvet in the following fashion: Lay the whole unsplit chicken breast on its side on a chopping board. Holding the breast firmly in place with one hand, cut it lengthwise along the curved breastbone with a cleaver or sharp knife. Carefully cut away all the meat from one side of the breastbone. Then grasp the meat in one hand and pull it off the bones and away from the skin—using the cleaver to free the meat if necessary. Turn the breast over and repeat on the other side. Remove each tube-shaped fillet from the rest of the breast meat, and pull out and discard the white tendon in each fillet. Chop the fillets coarsely into small bits. Holding the front of one main breast section, scrape the meat away from its membrane with repeated light strokes of the cleaver. Repeat with the other side of the breast.

Combine the breast meat with the fillets and then mince finely, adding about ¼ cup of water—a little at a time—as you work. Place the minced chicken in a mixing bowl, sprinkle it with the cornstarch and salt, and stir together gently but thoroughly with your hand or a large spoon. In a separate bowl, beat the egg whites with a fork or whisk until they are frothy, then pour them into the chicken mixture and mix thoroughly. The finished chicken velvet should be light and fluffy.

3. Have the bird's nest, chicken velvet, chicken stock, white pepper, cornstarch mixture and ham within easy reach.

TO COOK: In a 3- to 4-quart saucepan, bring the chicken stock to a boil over high heat. Drop in the bird's nest, bring to a boil again, then reduce the heat to low and simmer covered for 5 minutes. Add 1 teaspoon of salt and the white pepper. Give the cornstarch mixture a quick stir to recombine it and add it to the pan, stirring constantly and gently until the mixture thickens. Add the chicken velvet, stir once or twice to disperse it evenly through the soup and remove the pan from the heat. Pour the soup into a tureen, sprinkle the top with ham and serve at once.

Hün-t'un-t'ang
WONTON SOUP

餛飩湯

This is not the wonton soup you may have come upon in restaurants. The Chinese call this "soup wonton" and serve it as a substantial lunch. The serving of wontons in each portion makes this a full-meal soup.

To serve 4 to 6

THE WONTONS

1 recipe *wonton* wrappers, prepared according to directions on page 3, or ½ pound ready-made *wonton* wrappers, or 1 pound ready-made egg-roll wrappers cut into 3½-inch squares

¾ pound lean boneless pork, finely ground

4 teaspoons soy sauce

¾ teaspoon finely chopped, peeled fresh ginger root

¾ teaspoon salt

¾ pound fresh spinach, cooked, drained, squeezed dry and finely chopped, or 1 ten-ounce package chopped frozen spinach, defrosted, squeezed dry and chopped again (6 tablespoons after chopping)

THE SOUP

6 cups chicken stock, fresh or canned

1 cup loosely packed fresh watercress leaves, or 1 cup fresh spinach leaves, torn into very small pieces

PREPARE AHEAD: 1. To make the filling: In a large bowl, combine the pork, soy sauce, ginger and salt, and, using a spoon or your hands, mix them thoroughly. Then mix in the spinach.

2. To assemble the *wontons:* Place 1 teaspoon or so of the filling just below the center of each wrapper. Fold one side over the filling and tuck its edge under the filling. Then, with a finger dipped in water, moisten the exposed sides of the wrapper and roll up the filled cylinder, leaving ½ inch of wrapper unrolled at the top. Now take the two ends of the cylinder in the fingers of both hands and pull them down beneath the roll until the ends meet and overlap slightly. Pinch the ends firmly together. As each *wonton* is finished, place it on a plate and cover with a dry towel.

TO COOK: In a 4- to 5-quart saucepan, bring 2 quarts of water to a boil and drop in the *wontons*. Return to a boil, reduce the heat to moderate and cook uncovered for 5 minutes, or until tender but still a little resistant to the bite. Drain the *wontons* through a colander. Pour the stock into the pan and bring to a boil, add the watercress or spinach and the *wontons,* and return again to a boil. Serve at once.

Yü-ch'ih-t'ang

魚翅湯

SHARK'S FIN SOUP

To serve 6

4 ounces precooked and cleaned
  shark's fin
4 dried Chinese mushrooms, 1 to 1½
  inches in diameter
1 whole chicken breast, about ¾
  pound
4 cups chicken stock, fresh or canned,
  or cold water

1 teaspoon soy sauce
1½ teaspoons salt
⅛ teaspoon white pepper
2 tablespoons cornstarch, dissolved
  in 3 tablespoons cold chicken
  stock, fresh or canned, or cold
  water
1 slice Smithfield ham, ⅛ inch thick,
  cut into fine shreds 1½ to 2 inches
  long and ⅛ inch wide

PREPARE AHEAD: 1. In a small saucepan, cover the shark's fin with 4 cups of cold water and soak for at least 8 hours or overnight. Drain off the soaking water, add 4 cups of fresh cold water to the pan and bring to a boil over high heat. Reduce the heat to low and cook, uncovered, for 1 hour. Drain off the water, rinse the shark's fin well under cold running water and drain again.

2. In a small bowl, cover the mushrooms with ½ cup warm water and let them soak for 30 minutes. Remove them with a slotted spoon and discard the water. With a cleaver or sharp knife, cut away and discard the tough stems of the mushrooms and shred the caps by placing them, one at a time, flat on a chopping board, then cutting each of the caps into paper-thin slices horizontally. Cut the slices into the thinnest possible strips.

3. Bone, skin and shred the chicken breast in the following fashion: Lay the whole chicken breast on its side on a chopping board. Holding the breast firmly in place with your hand, cut it lengthwise through the skin, along the curved breastbone, with a cleaver or sharp knife. Carefully cut all the meat from the bones on one side of the breastbone. Then grasp the meat in one hand and pull it off the bones and away from the skin —using the cleaver to free the meat if necessary. Turn the breast over and repeat on the other side. Remove each tube-shaped fillet from the boned breast meat, and pull out and discard the white threadlike membranes. Lay the breast meat and fillets flat and cut them horizontally into paper-thin slices. Then cut the slices into shreds about 1½ to 2 inches long and ⅛ inch wide.

TO COOK: In a 3- to 4-quart saucepan, bring the chicken stock, shark's fin, soy sauce, salt and pepper to a boil over high heat, reduce the heat, and simmer, uncovered, for 30 minutes. Add the chicken and mushrooms, and stir thoroughly. Give the cornstarch mixture a quick stir to recombine it and add it to the soup. Cook, stirring constantly, until the soup thickens slightly. To serve, pour the soup into a tureen or individual soup bowls and garnish it with the ham. Serve at once.

Suan-la-t'ang
酸辣湯

SOUR-AND-HOT SOUP

To serve 4 to 6

4 dried Chinese mushrooms, 1 to 1½ inches in diameter
2 squares, 3 inches each, fresh Chinese bean curd, about ½ inch thick
½ cup canned bamboo shoots
¼ pound boneless pork
1 quart chicken stock, fresh or canned
1 teaspoon salt
1 tablespoon soy sauce
¼ teaspoon ground white pepper
2 tablespoons white vinegar
2 tablespoons cornstarch mixed with 3 tablespoons cold water
1 egg, lightly beaten
2 teaspoons sesame-seed oil
1 scallion, including the green top, finely chopped

PREPARE AHEAD: 1. In a small bowl, cover the mushrooms with ½ cup of warm water and let them soak for 30 minutes. Discard the water. With a cleaver or knife, cut away and discard the tough stems of the mushrooms, and shred the caps by placing one at a time on a chopping board. Cut them horizontally into paper-thin slices, and then into thin strips.

2. Drain the pieces of bamboo shoot and bean curd, and rinse them in cold water. Shred them as fine as the mushrooms.

3. With a cleaver or sharp knife, trim the pork of all fat. Then shred it, too, by slicing the meat as thin as possible and cutting the slices into narrow strips about 1½ to 2 inches long.

4. Have the above ingredients, stock, salt, soy sauce, pepper, vinegar, cornstarch mixture, egg, sesame-seed oil and scallions within easy reach.

TO COOK: Combine in a heavy 3-quart saucepan the stock, salt, soy sauce, mushrooms, bamboo shoots and pork. Bring to a boil over high heat, then immediately reduce the heat to low, cover the pan and simmer for 3 minutes. Drop in the bean curd, and the pepper and vinegar. Bring to a boil again. Give the cornstarch mixture a stir to recombine it and pour it into the soup. Stir for a few seconds until the soup thickens, then slowly pour in the beaten egg, stirring gently all the while. Remove the soup from the heat and ladle it into a tureen or serving bowl. Stir in the sesame-seed oil and sprinkle the top with scallions. Serve at once.

CHRYSANTHEMUM FIRE POT

To serve 6 to 8

4 ounces cellophane noodles
1 whole chicken breast, about ¾
　pound
½ pound lean, boneless pork
½ pound top sirloin of beef
½ pound calf's liver or chicken livers
½ pound raw shrimp in their shells
　(about 30-36 to a pound)
½ pound fillet of sole or pike
1 dozen small oysters, or small hard-

shell clams, shucked
1 pound celery cabbage
½ pound fresh, crisp spinach leaves
2 three-inch squares fresh bean curd,
　about ½ inch thick, cut into ½-
　inch-wide slices
¼ cup soy sauce
2 tablespoons sesame-seed oil
2 tablespoons Chinese rice wine, or
　pale dry sherry
3 eggs, lightly beaten
8 cups chicken stock, fresh or canned

PREPARE AHEAD: 1. Place the pork, beef, calf's liver or chicken livers and sole or pike in your freezer for about 30 minutes, or only long enough to firm the meat for easier slicing. Then, with a cleaver or sharp knife, cut the pork, beef, liver and fish horizontally into the thinnest possible slices. To make fairly uniform pieces that will be easy to handle with chopsticks, cut the slices into strips 3 inches long and 1 inch wide.

2. Bone, skin and slice the chicken breast in the following fashion: Lay the whole chicken breast on its side on a chopping board. Holding the breast firmly in place, cut it lengthwise along the curved breastbone with a cleaver or sharp knife. Carefully cut away all the meat from one side of the breastbone. Then grasp the meat in one hand and pull it off the bones and away from the skin—using the cleaver to free the meat if necessary. Turn the breast over and repeat on the other side. Remove each tube-shaped fillet from the boned breast meat, and pull out and discard the tendon in each fillet. Freeze the chicken for 30 minutes to firm it. Then lay the breast meat and fillets flat, and cut them horizontally into paper-thin slices. Then cut the slices crosswise into pieces 3 inches wide and 1 inch long.

3. In a large, flat pan or dish, cover the cellophane noodles with 2 cups of warm water and soak them for 30 minutes. Then drain the noodles and cut them into 6-inch lengths.

4. Shell the shrimp. With a small, sharp knife, make a shallow incision down their backs and lift out the black or white intestinal vein with the point of the knife. Slice the shrimp in half, lengthwise.

5. With a cleaver or sharp knife, cut away any wilted leaves from the cabbage and separate it into stalks. Wash the stalks under cold water and cut each stalk into 1-by-3-inch pieces. Blanch the cabbage by dropping the pieces into a pot of boiling water. Immediately turn off the heat. Let the cabbage pieces rest in the water for 3 minutes, then drain and pat them dry.

6. Trim the spinach leaves of their stalks and wash the leaves thoroughly.

7. Arrange each kind of meat, fish or seafood, and the noodles and veg-

etables in overlapping layers on plates or in separate rows on 2 large platters.

8. Mix the soy sauce, sesame-seed oil and wine in a small bowl, and stir in the eggs. Mix thoroughly, then ladle a tablespoon of the sauce into 6 individual soup bowls, and pour the rest into a serving bowl.

9. Have the above ingredients and the chicken stock within easy reach.

TO COOK: If you have a fire pot, preheat the broiler to its highest point. Arrange 20 charcoal briquets side by side in a baking pan lined with heavy aluminum foil and place it under the broiler. Heat for 10 to 15 minutes until a white ash forms on the briquets. With tongs, transfer the briquets to the funnel of the fire pot. Lay an asbestos mat in the center of the dining table and carefully set the fire pot on it.

If you do not have a fire pot, substitute an electric casserole set at 300°. In a 3- to 4-quart saucepan, bring the chicken stock to a bubbling boil, then pour it into the fire pot (or electric casserole). Keep the stock simmering throughout the meal. Arrange the plates or platters of uncooked food around the fire pot and give each guest a bowl of sauce. Place the extra sauce in its bowl on the table. Traditionally, each guest picks up a piece of food from the platters with chopsticks and transfers it to a wire strainer to cook in the simmering stock. When cooked to taste, it is plucked out of the strainer with chopsticks, dipped into sauce and eaten. The strainer may be eliminated and the food held in the stock with chopsticks. Or long-handled forks with heatproof handles may be used—fondue forks if available. When all the meat, fish and seafood have been consumed, a little of the stock (now a rich, highly flavored broth) is ladled into each guest's bowl and drunk as a soup. The noodles and vegetables are then dropped into the stock remaining in the fire pot, cooked for a minute or so, and ladled with the broth into the bowls to be eaten as a last course.

Tan-hua-t'ang   蛋花湯
EGG DROP SOUP

To serve 4

3 cups chicken stock, fresh or canned
1 teaspoon salt
1 tablespoon cornstarch dissolved in

2 tablespoons chicken stock, fresh or canned, or cold water
1 egg lightly beaten
1 scallion, including the green top, finely chopped

TO COOK: Over high heat, bring the chicken stock to a boil in a 2-quart saucepan and add the salt. Give the cornstarch mixture a quick stir to recombine it, and add it to the pan, stirring for a few seconds until the stock thickens slightly and becomes clear. Slowly pour in the egg and stir once gently. Immediately turn off the heat. Taste and add more salt if needed. Pour the soup into a tureen or individual bowls, garnish with the chopped scallions and serve at once.

Shua-yang-jou

涮羊肉

MONGOLIAN FIRE POT (RINSED LAMB)

To serve 6

3 pounds lean, boneless lamb, cut
from the leg or shoulder
4 ounces cellophane noodles
½ pound fresh, crisp spinach
½ pound celery cabbage
½ cup soy sauce
2 tablespoons sesame-seed oil
2 tablespoons Chinese rice wine, or
pale dry sherry
1 tablespoon brown sugar dissolved
in 1 tablespoon boiling water
2 tablespoons smooth peanut butter,
thinned with 4 tablespoons boiling
water

¼ teaspoon cayenne pepper
1 tablespoon fermented red bean
curd, mashed
8 to 10 cups chicken stock, fresh or
canned
2 scallions, white part only, finely
chopped
1 teaspoon finely chopped garlic
1 tablespoon finely chopped, peeled
fresh ginger root
¼ cup finely chopped Chinese parsley
(*cilantro*), or substitute flat-leaf
parsley
Steamed flower rolls, prepared
according to the recipe on page 9

PREPARE AHEAD: 1. Place the lamb in the freezer for 2 or 3 hours, or
only long enough to firm it for easier slicing. Then, with a cleaver or
heavy, sharp knife, cut the lamb against the grain into paper-thin slices.
(Or ask your butcher to slice the lamb for you.) Cut the slices into 2-by-3-
inch pieces. Divide the lamb into 6 equal portions (½ pound of meat
per person) and arrange the pieces in an overlapping row or circle on individual plates.

2. In a large, flat pan or dish, cover the cellophane noodles with 2
cups of warm water and let them soak for 30 minutes. Then drain and
cut the noodles into 6-inch lengths. Place on a platter.

3. Trim the spinach leaves of their tough stalks, wash the leaves thoroughly under cold running water and drain. Pat them dry with paper towels and arrange them on the platter with the noodles.

4. With a cleaver or sharp knife, trim off the wilted greens and the root
ends of the cabbage. Separate the cabbage into stalks and wash under
cold running water. Cut each stalk into 1-by-3-inch pieces and blanch
them by dropping them into a pot of boiling water. Let them rest in the
water for 2 to 3 minutes, then drain, pat dry with paper towels, and place
on the platter with the spinach and noodles.

5. In a large bowl, combine the soy sauce, sesame-seed oil, wine, di-
luted brown sugar, the thinned peanut butter, cayenne pepper and red
bean curd. Mix thoroughly, then ladle 1 tablespoon of the sauce into
each of 6 individual soup bowls. Pour the rest into a small serving bowl.

6. Have the above ingredients, and the chicken stock, scallions, garlic, ginger and parsley within easy reach. Reheat the steamed flower rolls and keep them warm.

TO COOK: Prepare the fire pot or whatever substitute pot you have chosen, as described in the recipe for the chrysanthemum fire pot *(page 26)*.

In a 3- to 4-quart saucepan, bring the chicken stock to a boil, then pour it into the fire pot or electric casserole. Place the platter of noodles, Chinese cabbage and spinach, the steamed flower rolls and the bowl of extra sauce next to the pot. Give each guest a plate of lamb and a soup bowl. Drop the scallions, garlic, ginger and parsley into the boiling stock. Each guest then cooks his own lamb, as described in the recipe for the chrysanthemum fire pot. When all the lamb has been consumed, a little of the stock (now a rich, highly flavored broth) is ladled into each guest's bowl and served as a soup. The noodles and vegetables are then dropped into the stock remaining in the fire pot, cooked for a minute or so and ladled with the broth into the bowls as a last course.

Tung-kua-t'ang 冬 瓜 湯
WINTER MELON SOUP

To serve 4

6 small dried Chinese mushrooms, ½
   to 1 inch in diameter
1 pound of winter melon

3 cups chicken stock, fresh or canned
A ⅛-inch-thick slice cooked
   Smithfield ham, cut into 1- to 1½-
   inch pieces

PREPARE AHEAD: 1. In a small bowl, cover the mushrooms with ½ cup of warm water and soak them for 30 minutes. Discard the water. Cut away the stems of the mushrooms.

2. Peel the melon, and discard the inner seeds and stringy fibers. Cut the melon pulp into ¼-inch slices, then cut the slices into 1- to 1½-inch pieces.

3. Have the mushrooms, melon, stock and ham within easy reach.

TO COOK: In a 2- to 3-quart heavy saucepan, combine the chicken stock, melon and mushrooms, and bring to a boil. Reduce the heat to low, cover the pan and simmer for 15 minutes. To serve, ladle the soup into a tureen or serving bowl and stir in the pieces of ham.

TEN-VARIETIES HOT POT

To serve 6 to 8

8 dried Chinese mushrooms, 1 to 1½ inches in diameter

2 ounces cellophane noodles

½ pound Chinese cabbage, celery cabbage or *bok choy*

1 pound fresh spinach leaves, washed and torn into small pieces

12 bamboo shoot slices (⅛ inch thick) cut into tree shapes according to directions on page 69 of the main volume

2 slices (⅛ inch thick) cooked Smithfield ham, cut into 2½-by-1-inch pieces

12 shrimp balls, prepared according to the recipe on page 57

12 slices (2½-by-1-by-⅛-inch) star anise beef, prepared according to the recipe on page 79

12 slices (2½-by-1-by-⅛-inch) roast pork, prepared according to the recipe on page 65

12 slices (½ inch thick) egg pancake with pork filling, prepared according to the recipe on page 103

6 cups chicken stock, fresh or canned

¼ cup soy sauce

1 tablespoon sesame-seed oil

PREPARE AHEAD: 1. In a small bowl, soak the mushrooms in ½ cup of warm water for 30 minutes. Discard the water. With a cleaver or knife, cut away and discard the tough stems of the mushrooms, and cut each cap in half.

2. In another bowl, soak the noodles in 2 cups of warm water for 30 minutes. Drain, discard the water and cut the noodles into 4-inch lengths.

3. With a cleaver or sharp knife, trim any wilted green leaves and the root ends off the cabbage. Separate the stalks, wash them under cold water and cut them lengthwise into strips 3 inches long by 1 inch wide. Blanch the strips in 2 quarts of boiling water for 1 minute, then drain them thoroughly.

4. In a large bowl, combine the soy sauce and sesame-seed oil, and mix thoroughly. Then ladle the sauce into 6 or 8 individual soup bowls.

5. Have the above ingredients, spinach, ham, shrimp balls, star anise beef, roast pork, egg pancake slices and chicken stock within easy reach.

TO COOK: Prepare the fire pot as described in the recipe for the chrysanthemum fire pot *(page 26)*, or substitute a chafing dish, fondue pot or electric casserole.

Place the cabbage, spinach and noodles in the fire pot or whatever utensil you are using, in one layer, and on top of them arrange the ham, shrimp balls, beef, mushrooms, pancake slices, pork and bamboo shoots. Pour the stock in along the side of the pot, trying not to disturb the pattern of the food. Bring to a boil, cover the pot and cook for 10 minutes.

Give each guest a bowl of dipping sauce and either chopsticks, a long heatproof-handled fork or a fondue fork, and let them help themselves from the pot. When all the food is consumed, ladle the remaining stock into soup bowls and serve it as a final course.

Vegetables and Salads

Hsien-ts'ai-ts'an-tou

鹹菜蠶豆

STIR-FRIED BEANS WITH PICKLED MUSTARD GREENS

To serve 4 to 6

1½ pounds fresh lima beans, shelled (1½ cups), or 1 ten-ounce package of frozen baby lima beans, thoroughly defrosted, or use shelled and peeled fresh *fava* beans
1 cup pickled mustard greens, or substitute good-quality fresh sauerkraut
3 tablespoons peanut oil, or flavorless vegetable oil
2 teaspoons sugar
½ teaspoon salt
½ cup chicken stock, fresh or canned

PREPARE AHEAD: 1. Blanch the fresh lima or *fava* beans in 1 quart of boiling water by cooking them over high heat for 10 minutes—15 minutes if they are large. Drain thoroughly. Frozen beans need only be thoroughly defrosted.

2. Place the pickled mustard greens or sauerkraut in a sieve and wash well under cold running water. Pat dry with paper towels, then, with a cleaver or sharp knife, chop the greens or sauerkraut as fine as possible.

3. Have the above ingredients, the oil, sugar, salt and chicken stock within easy reach.

TO COOK: Set a 12-inch wok or 10-inch skillet over high heat for 30 seconds. Pour in 2 tablespoons of the oil, swirl it about in the pan and heat for another 30 seconds, turning the heat down to moderate if the oil begins to smoke. Add the mustard greens or sauerkraut and stir-fry over moderate heat for 2 minutes. Add the sugar, mix well, then transfer the greens to a plate. Pour the remaining tablespoon of oil into the pan and drop in the beans. Stir-fry over low heat for 4 or 5 minutes before adding the chicken stock and salt. Bring to a boil, then lower the heat again and simmer the beans, covered, for about 5 minutes, or until they are tender. Return the mustard greens or sauerkraut to the pan and stir together only long enough to heat them through. Transfer the entire contents of the pan to a heated platter and serve at once.

Chao-chieh-ts'ai

炒芥菜

STIR-FRIED BROCCOLI

To serve 6

A 2-pound bunch of broccoli
2 tablespoons peanut oil, or flavorless
vegetable oil
1 teaspoon salt

½ teaspoon sugar
2 tablespoons chicken stock, fresh or
canned
1 teaspoon cornstarch dissolved in 1
tablespoon chicken stock, fresh or
canned, or cold water

PREPARE AHEAD: 1. Wash the broccoli under cold running water. With a small, sharp knife, cut the broccoli flowerets from their stems in fairly large clusters. Place them in a bowl. Peel the stems by cutting about ⅛ inch into the stringy skin and stripping it down as if you were peeling an onion. Slice the stalks diagonally into 1-inch pieces, discarding the tough, woody ends. Place the pieces of stalk in a separate bowl.

2. Have the broccoli, and the salt, sugar, stock and cornstarch mixture within easy reach.

TO COOK: Set a 12-inch wok or 10-inch skillet over medium heat for 30 seconds. Pour in the 2 tablespoons of oil, swirl it about in the pan and heat for another 30 seconds, lowering the heat to moderate if the oil begins to smoke. Drop in the broccoli stalks and stir-fry for about 1 minute to coat the vegetable pieces thoroughly with oil. Add the broccoli flowerets and stir-fry for 1 more minute. Sprinkle in the salt and sugar, and add the chicken broth, stirring for a few seconds. Then cover the pan and cook over moderate heat for 2 to 3 minutes; the broccoli should be tender but still crisp. Give the cornstarch mixture a quick stir to recombine it and pour it into the pan. Stir for a few seconds until the broccoli is coated with a light, clear glaze. Transfer to a heated platter and serve at once.

Chao-ssŭ-chi-tou

炒四季豆

STIR-FRIED STRING BEANS AND WATER CHESTNUTS

To serve 4

1 pound fresh string beans
2 tablespoons peanut oil, or
flavorless vegetable oil
1½ teaspoons salt
1 teaspoon sugar

10 water chestnuts, cut into ¼-inch
slices
¼ cup chicken stock, fresh or canned
1 teaspoon cornstarch dissolved in 1
tablespoon chicken stock, fresh or
canned

PREPARE AHEAD: 1. Snap off and discard the ends of the beans, and, with a small knife, remove any strings. Cut the beans into 2-inch pieces.

2. Have the beans, oil, salt, sugar, water chestnuts, chicken stock and cornstarch mixture within easy reach.

TO COOK: Set a 12-inch wok or 10-inch skillet over high heat for 30 seconds. Pour in the 2 tablespoons of oil, swirl it about in the pan and heat for another 30 seconds, turning the heat down to moderate if the oil begins to smoke. Drop in the string beans and stir-fry for 3 minutes. Add the salt, sugar and water chestnuts, and stir once or twice before pouring in the stock. Cover the pan and cook over moderate heat for 2 to 3 minutes until the beans are tender but still crisp. Now give the cornstarch mixture a stir to recombine it and add it to the pan. Cook, stirring, until the vegetables are coated with a light, clear glaze. Transfer the entire contents of the pan to a heated platter and serve at once.

Chao-hsüeh-tou   炒雪豆

STIR-FRIED SNOW PEAS WITH CHINESE MUSHROOMS AND BAMBOO SHOOTS

To serve 4

6 dried Chinese mushrooms, 1 to 1½ inches in diameter
1 pound fresh snow peas (thoroughly defrosted frozen snow peas will do, but they will not have the crispness of the fresh ones)

½ cup canned bamboo shoots, sliced ⅛ inch thick and cut into 1-by-1-inch triangular tree-shaped pieces
1½ teaspoons salt
½ teaspoon sugar
2 tablespoons peanut oil, or flavorless vegetable oil

PREPARE AHEAD: 1. In a small bowl, cover the mushrooms with ½ cup of warm water and let them soak for 30 minutes. Remove them with a slotted spoon. With a cleaver or sharp knife, cut away and discard the tough stems of the mushrooms and cut each cap into quarters. Strain the soaking water through a fine sieve and reserve 2 tablespoons of it.

2. Snap off the tips of the fresh snow peas and remove the strings from the pea pods.

3. Have the above ingredients, and the oil, bamboo shoots, salt and sugar within easy reach.

TO COOK: Set a 12-inch wok or 10-inch skillet over high heat for 30 seconds. Pour in the 2 tablespoons of oil, swirl it about in the pan and heat for another 30 seconds, turning the heat down to moderate if the oil begins to smoke. Immediately drop in the mushrooms and bamboo shoots, and stir-fry for 2 minutes. Add the snow peas, salt and sugar, and then 2 tablespoons of the reserved mushroom-soaking water. Cook, stirring constantly at high heat, for about 2 minutes, or until the water evaporates. Transfer the contents of the pan to a heated platter and serve at once.

La-pai-ts'ai

辣白菜

STIR-FRIED SPICED CABBAGE

To serve 4

1 pound Chinese cabbage, celery
   cabbage or *bok choy*, or substitute
   green cabbage
2 tablespoons sugar

2 tablespoons white vinegar
1 tablespoon soy sauce
1 teaspoon salt
¼ teaspoon cayenne pepper
1 tablespoon peanut oil, or flavorless
   vegetable oil

PREPARE AHEAD: 1. With a cleaver or sharp knife, trim the top leaves of the cabbage and the root ends. Separate the stalks and wash them under cold running water. Cut each stalk, leaves and all, into 1-by-1½-inch pieces. If you are substituting green cabbage, separate the leaves and wash in cold water. Then cut the leaves into 1-by-1½-inch pieces.

2. In a small bowl, combine the sugar, vinegar, soy sauce, salt and cayenne pepper, and mix thoroughly. Have the oil within easy reach.

TO COOK: Set a 12-inch wok or 10-inch skillet over high heat for about 30 seconds. Pour in the oil, swirl it about in the pan and heat for another 30 seconds, then turn the heat down to moderate. Immediately add the cabbage and stir-fry for 2 to 3 minutes. Make sure all the cabbage is coated with the oil. Remove the pan from the heat and stir in the soy-vinegar mixture. Transfer the cabbage to a platter and let it cool to lukewarm before serving. Or, if you prefer, serve it chilled.

Chao-ou-pien

炒藕片

STIR-FRIED LOTUS ROOT, CHINESE MUSHROOMS AND BAMBOO SHOOTS

To serve 4

4 dried Chinese mushrooms, 1 to 1½
   inches in diameter
2 cups canned lotus root
½ cup thinly sliced canned bamboo
   shoots

2 tablespoons peanut oil, or flavorless
   vegetable oil
1½ teaspoons salt
½ teaspoon sugar

PREPARE AHEAD: 1. In a small bowl, cover the mushrooms with ½ cup of warm water and let them soak for 30 minutes. Remove them with a slotted spoon and save the water. With a cleaver or sharp knife, cut off and discard the tough stems of the mushrooms and quarter each cap.

2. Drain the canned lotus root and rinse it under cold water. Cut it into ⅛ inch slices.

3. Have the above ingredients, bamboo shoots, oil, salt and sugar within easy reach.

TO COOK: Set a 12-inch wok or 10-inch skillet over high heat for 30 seconds. Pour in the 2 tablespoons of oil, swirl it about in the pan and heat for another 30 seconds, turning the heat down to moderate if the oil begins to smoke. Add the lotus root and stir-fry for 1 minute, or until all the pieces are thoroughly coated with the oil. Add the mushrooms, bamboo shoots, salt, sugar and ¼ cup of mushroom-soaking water. Stir thoroughly and cover the pan. Cook over low heat for 5 minutes, then transfer the entire contents of the pan to a heated platter and serve at once.

VARIATION: A 1-pound head of green cabbage may be substituted for the canned lotus root. Wash the cabbage, core it and separate the leaves. Then, with a cleaver or sharp knife, cut the leaves into strips about 1 inch long and ½ inch wide.

Hung-shao-ch'ieh-tzŭ   紅燒茄子
BRAISED EGGPLANT WITH DRIED SHRIMP

To serve 4 to 6

	vegetable oil
¼ cup dried shrimp	1 tablespoon soy sauce
1 medium eggplant, about 1 pound	1 tablespoon Chinese rice wine, or
8 medium garlic cloves, unpeeled	pale dry sherry
4 tablespoons peanut oil, or flavorless	1 teaspoon sugar

PREPARE AHEAD: 1. In a small bowl, cover the dried shrimp with ½ cup of warm water and let them soak for 30 minutes. Do not discard the soaking water.

2. Wash the eggplant under cold running water, then cut it, unpeeled, from top to bottom into long ½-inch-thick slices. Cut the slices into strips about 2 inches long and ½ inch wide.

3. Crush each garlic clove by placing the flat of a cleaver over it and giving it a sharp blow with your fist. Remove and discard the peel.

4. Have the above ingredients, and the oil, soy sauce, wine and sugar within easy reach.

TO COOK: Set a 12-inch wok or 10-inch skillet over moderate heat for 30 seconds. Pour in 4 tablespoons of oil, swirl it about in the pan and heat for 30 seconds longer. Add the garlic and eggplant, turn the heat down to low and cook, stirring frequently, for 15 minutes, or until lightly browned. Add the soy sauce, wine, sugar, shrimp and shrimp water. Cover the pan and cook, still over low heat, for 10 minutes, or until all the liquid has been absorbed. Transfer to a platter and serve either hot or cold. Although the garlic is usually served with the eggplant and shrimp, it may be removed if you prefer.

Ma-p'o-tou-fu
STIR-FRIED SPICED BEAN CURD AND PORK

麻婆豆腐

¼ pound lean fresh pork, finely
  ground
1 tablespoon soy sauce
1 tablespoon Chinese rice wine, or
  pale dry sherry
½ teaspoon sugar
¼ teaspoon Szechwan peppercorns
3 tablespoons peanut oil, or flavorless
  vegetable oil
4 pieces (3-inch square) fresh bean
  curd, about ½ inch thick
1 tablespoon brown-bean sauce

¼ teaspoon cayenne pepper
1 teaspoon chopped, peeled fresh
  ginger root
2 scallions, white part only, finely
  chopped
¼ cup chicken stock, fresh or canned
1 teaspoon salt
2 teaspoons cornstarch dissolved in
  1 tablespoon cold chicken stock,
  fresh or canned, or cold water
2 teaspoons sesame-seed oil

PREPARE AHEAD: 1. In a bowl, combine the pork, soy sauce, wine and sugar. With a spoon, mix them together well.

2. Set a small wok or 10-inch skillet over high heat and drop in the Szechwan peppercorns. Turn the heat to medium and cook, stirring constantly, for about 5 minutes, or until they are lightly browned. Then crush the peppercorns to a fine powder with a mortar and pestle or wrap them in a kitchen towel and crush them with a rolling pin. Shake through a strainer into a small bowl and set aside.

3. Have the oil, bean curd, bean sauce, cayenne pepper, ginger, scallions, chicken stock, salt, cornstarch mixture and seasame-seed oil within easy reach.

TO COOK: Set a 12-inch wok or 10-inch skillet over high heat for 30 seconds. Pour in the 3 tablespoons of oil, swirl it about in the pan and heat for another 30 seconds, turning the heat down to moderate if the oil begins to smoke. Drop in the pork mixture and stir-fry for about 2 to 3 minutes, or until the pork is no longer pink. Add the bean curd, bean sauce, hot pepper, ginger, scallions, chicken stock and salt, and cook over moderate heat for 2 to 3 minutes. Give the cornstarch mixture a quick stir to recombine it and add it to the pan. Cook, stirring constantly, until the sauce is lightly thickened and clear. Then add the Szechwan pepper and sesame-seed oil, transfer the entire contents of the pan to a heated platter and serve at once. As a main course, this will serve 2. As part of a Chinese meal *(page 120)*, it will serve 2 to 4.

Lo-po-hsien-ko

蘿蔔鮮蛤

STIR-FRIED ICICLE RADISH WITH CLAMS

To serve 4 to 6

1 pound Chinese icicle radish
1 dozen fresh hard-shell clams in their
   shells, preferably cherrystone or
   littleneck clams
2 teaspoons cornstarch, dissolved in
   2 tablespoons clam juice

2 tablespoons peanut oil, or flavorless
   vegetable oil
1 scallion, including the green top,
   finely chopped
1 teaspoon salt
1 teaspoon sugar

PREPARE AHEAD: 1. With a small knife, peel off and discard the thick skin of the radish, and cut the radish crosswise into ⅛-inch slices. Then cut the slices into shreds 2 inches long and ⅛ inch wide. (There should be about 3 cups.)

2. Shuck the clams, or have the fishmonger do it for you. To rid the clam juice of sand, strain it through a double layer of cheesecloth into a small bowl. Put aside ½ cup of the clam juice into one bowl and dissolve the cornstarch in an additional 2 tablespoons of clam juice in another bowl. Cut the clams in half, washing them in cold water if they seem sandy. Reserve them in a third bowl.

3. Have the above ingredients, the oil, scallions, salt and sugar within easy reach.

TO COOK: Set a 12-inch wok or 10-inch skillet over high heat for about 30 seconds. Pour in 2 tablespoons of oil, swirl it about in the pan and heat for another 30 seconds, turning the heat down to moderate if the oil begins to smoke. Add the scallions, stir-fry for a few seconds, then drop in the shredded radish. Stir-fry for 2 minutes. Add the salt and sugar. Pour in the ½ cup of clam juice, bring to a boil and cover the pan. Reduce the heat to moderate and cook for 10 minutes. Then drop in the clams, stir for 30 seconds—no longer, or they will toughen. Give the cornstarch mixture a quick stir to recombine it and pour it over the clams. Stir over high heat for a few seconds until all the ingredients are coated with a light, clear glaze. Transfer the entire contents of the pan to a heated platter and serve at once.

Su-shih-chin

TEN-VARIETIES VEGETARIAN DISH

To serve 4 to 6

20 dried tiger lily buds

1 tablespoon dried cloud ears

6 dried Chinese mushrooms, 1 to
1½ inches in diameter

2 ounces cellophane noodles

½ pound Chinese cabbage (celery
cabbage or *bok choy*)

¼ pound fresh snow peas or
substitute ½ cup thoroughly
defrosted frozen snow peas

3 tablespoons peanut oil, or flavorless
vegetable oil

½ cup canned bamboo shoots, sliced
⅛ inch thick and cut into 1-inch
squares

6 fresh peeled water chestnuts or
drained canned water chestnuts

20 canned gingko nuts

½ cup canned vegetable steak, cut
into 1-inch squares

1 tablespoon soy sauce

1 teaspoon salt

¼ teaspoon monosodium glutamate

1 cup water

1 tablespoon sesame-seed oil

PREPARE AHEAD: 1. In a small bowl, combine the tiger lily buds and cloud ears, and cover them with 2 cups of warm water. Let them soak for 30 minutes. Drain and discard the water. Wash the lilies and cloud ears well under cold running water. Then cut away and discard the hard ends of the tiger lilies and cut the lilies in two. Break the cloud ears into small pieces.

2. Cover the dried mushrooms with ½ cup of warm water in another bowl and let them soak for 30 minutes. Drain them and save the water. With a cleaver or sharp knife, cut away and discard the tough stems. Slice the mushroom caps in quarters.

3. Cover the cellophane noodles with 2 cups of warm water in another bowl and soak for 30 minutes. Drain. Cut the noodles into 4-inch lengths.

4. With a cleaver or sharp knife, trim off the wilted top leaves and the root ends of the cabbage and separate it into stalks. Wash the stalks under cold running water and cut them into strips 1½ inches long and ½ inch wide.

5. Break off the tips of the fresh snow peas and discard. Remove stringy edges from the pea pods.

6. Have the above vegetables, and the oil, bamboo shoots, water chestnuts, gingko nuts, vegetable steak, soy sauce, salt, monosodium glutamate, water and sesame-seed oil within easy reach.

TO COOK: Set a 12-inch wok or 10-inch skillet over high heat for about 30 seconds. Pour in the 3 tablespoons of oil, swirl it about in the pan and heat for another 30 seconds, turning the heat down to moderate if the oil begins to smoke. Add the cabbage and stir-fry for about 2 minutes. Then add the tiger lilies, cloud ears, mushrooms, cellophane noodles, snow peas, bamboo shoots, water chestnuts, gingko nuts and vegetable steak. Stir-fry for 2 minutes, and pour in the soy sauce, salt, monosodium glutamate and water. Let the stock come to a boil, then cover the pan and reduce the heat to low. Simmer for 10 minutes. Add the sesame-seed oil and mix thoroughly. Transfer the entire contents of the pan to a heated platter and serve at once.

Nai-yu-ts'ai-hsin   奶 油 菜 心
CREAMED CHINESE CABBAGE

To serve 4

1 pound Chinese cabbage (*bok choy* or celery cabbage)
1½ tablespoons cornstarch
¼ cup cold milk

2 tablespoons rendered chicken fat
1 teaspoon salt
¼ teaspoon sugar
¾ cup chicken stock, fresh or canned
A ⅛-inch slice cooked Smithfield ham, finely chopped

PREPARE AHEAD: 1. With a cleaver or sharp knife, trim off the wilted leaves and root ends of the cabbage. Separate the stalks and wash them under cold running water. If you are using *bok choy,* cut it crosswise into 1-inch slices; if you are using celery cabbage, cut it into 1-by-2-inch pieces.

2. Combine the cornstarch and milk in a small bowl, and stir with a spoon until the cornstarch is thoroughly dissolved.

3. Have the above ingredients, the chicken fat, salt, sugar, chicken stock and ham within easy reach.

TO COOK: Set a 12-inch wok or 10-inch skillet over high heat for about 30 seconds. Add the chicken fat, swirl it about in the pan and heat for another 30 seconds, turning the heat down to moderate if the fat begins to smoke. Add the *bok choy* and stir-fry over moderate heat for about 1 minute, or until the cabbage pieces are thoroughly coated with the fat. Sprinkle with salt and sugar, then pour in the chicken stock and stir well. Bring the stock to a boil and cover the pan. Turn the heat to low and simmer the cabbage undisturbed for 10 minutes, or until it is tender. With a slotted spoon, transfer the cabbage to a heated platter and, raising the heat, bring the cooking liquid in the pan to a boil. Give the cornstarch mixture a quick stir to recombine it and add it to the pan. Stir until the sauce thickens. Pour it over the waiting cabbage, sprinkle with the chopped ham and serve at once.

T'ang-ts'u-ou-pien

糖醋藕片

FRESH LOTUS ROOT SALAD

To serve 4 to 6

1 pound fresh lotus root
1 tablespoon soy sauce

1 tablespoon white vinegar
1 tablespoon sugar
2 teaspoons sesame-seed oil
½ teaspoon salt

PREPARE AHEAD: 1. Wash the fresh lotus root under cold running water and, with a sharp knife, peel off the skin. Trim off and discard both ends of the root.

2. With a cleaver or sharp knife, cut the lotus root into ⅛-inch-thick slices, dropping the slices as you proceed into a saucepan of cold water to prevent them from discoloring. Drain off the cold water and pour 3 to 4 cups of boiling water over the lotus root slices to cover them completely. Let them soak for 5 minutes. Drain the slices again, rinse them thoroughly under cold running water and then pat the slices completely dry with paper towels.

3. In a small mixing bowl, combine the soy sauce, vinegar, sugar, sesame-seed oil and salt, and stir them together until the sugar and salt are dissolved.

TO ASSEMBLE: Arrange the slices of lotus root, overlapping them in concentric circles on a serving plate. Pour the soy sauce-vinegar dressing evenly over the slices. Chill the salad in the refrigerator for at least 1 hour before serving.

Liang-pan-huang-kua

涼拌黄瓜

CUCUMBER SALAD WITH SPICY DRESSING

2 medium cucumbers
1 teaspoon soy sauce
1 tablespoon white vinegar
1 tablespoon sugar

2 teaspoons sesame-seed oil
¼ teaspoon Tabasco
½ teaspoon salt

Peel the cucumbers and cut them lengthwise in two. With a small spoon, scrape the seeds out of each half, leaving hollow boatlike shells. Cut the cucumbers crosswise into ¼-inch slices. In a small glass or porcelain bowl, combine the soy sauce, vinegar, sugar, sesame-seed oil, Tabasco and salt, and mix well. Add the cucumber. With a large spoon, toss to coat each slice thoroughly with the dressing. Chill slightly before serving. As a separate salad, this will serve 3 or 4. As a cold side dish at a Chinese meal, it will serve 4 to 6.

Liang-pan-hsi-yang-ts'ai 涼拌西洋菜
WATERCRESS AND WATER CHESTNUT SALAD

To serve 4

2 bunches watercress
8 peeled fresh water chestnuts or
    drained canned water chestnuts

1 teaspoon soy sauce
2 teaspoons sesame-seed oil
½ teaspoon salt
1 teaspoon sugar

PREPARE AHEAD: 1. With a small knife, trim and discard the tough ends of the watercress stems. Wash the watercress under cold running water, drop it into a pot of boiling water, then drain and pat the leaves dry with paper towels. With a cleaver or large knife, chop the watercress fine.

2. Wash the water chestnuts, drain and cut them into ⅛-inch slices. Then chop them fine.

TO ASSEMBLE: Combine in a large bowl the soy sauce, sesame-seed oil, salt and sugar, and mix thoroughly. Add the watercress and water chestnuts, and toss them well with a large spoon so that they are well coated with the mixture. Chill and serve.

Hsia-mi-pan-ch'in-ts'ai 蝦米拌芹菜
CELERY AND DRIED-SHRIMP SALAD

To serve 4 to 6

1 bunch celery
20 Chinese dried shrimp
1 tablespoon Chinese rice wine, or
    pale dry sherry

1 tablespoon warm water
1 teaspoon soy sauce
½ teaspoon salt
1 tablespoon sugar
1 tablespoon white vinegar
2 teaspoons sesame-seed oil

PREPARE AHEAD: 1. Wash the shrimp under cold running water. In a small bowl, combine them with the wine and 1 tablespoon of warm water. Let them marinate for 30 minutes. Drain, saving the marinade.

2. Remove and discard the leaves of the celery and any stringy stalks. Cut the stalks lengthwise in two, then crosswise into 1-inch pieces.

TO ASSEMBLE: In a large glass bowl, combine the reserved shrimp marinade, soy sauce, salt, sugar, vinegar and sesame-seed oil, and stir until the sugar dissolves. Add the shrimp and celery, and toss them about until they are coated with the dressing. Chill for 1 hour before serving.

Liang-pan-lu-sün

涼拌蘆筍

FRESH ASPARAGUS SALAD

1½ to 2 pounds of young, fresh
   asparagus, each stalk no more than
   ½ inch in diameter

4 teaspoons soy sauce
1 teaspoon sugar
2 teaspoons sesame-seed oil

PREPARE AHEAD: 1. Bend each asparagus stalk back until the tough root end snaps away. Discard the ends. Slice the remaining stalks in 1½-inch lengths, using the roll-cut method: that is, making a diagonal slice through one end of the stalk, then rolling the stalk a quarter turn and slicing again. There should be about 3 cups of asparagus pieces.

2. Wash the asparagus under cold running water and parboil the pieces by dropping them into 2 quarts of rapidly boiling water for 1 minute. Drain at once, and run cold water over the asparagus to stop their cooking and set their color. Spread them on a double thickness of paper towels and pat them completely dry.

TO ASSEMBLE: In a small glass bowl, combine the soy sauce, sugar and sesame-seed oil, and mix until the sugar is completely dissolved. Add the asparagus. With a large spoon, toss to coat each asparagus piece thoroughly with the dressing. Chill slightly—no longer than 2 hours—before serving. As a separate salad course, this will serve 4. As part of a Chinese meal (*page 120*), it will serve 6 to 8.

T'ang-yen-hung-lo-po

糖腌紅蘿蔔

MARINATED RADISH FANS

24 crisp red radishes, about 1 inch in
   diameter

1 teaspoon salt
1 tablespoon sugar

PREPARE AHEAD: 1. With a small, sharp knife, cut away and discard the root and stalk ends of each radish. Wash them under cold running water. Then lay each radish on its side and make parallel cuts along its entire upper surface about 1⁄16 of an inch apart and 2⁄3 of the way down. Be careful not to cut all the way through the radish.

2. Pour 1 teaspoon of salt and 1 tablespoon of sugar into a 1-quart glass jar. Add the radishes, cover the jar and shake vigorously so that each radish is coated with the mixture. Marinate at room temperature for at least 6 hours or overnight.

TO SERVE: Pour off all the liquid that will have accumulated in the jar and remove the radishes. The radishes will now be soft and pliable, and can be spread out to form decorative fan shapes. These are used traditionally to garnish cold dishes or salads.

Noodles and Rice

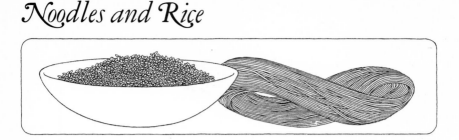

Pai-fan

白飯

CHINESE BOILED RICE

To serve 4

1 cup long-grain white rice	1¾ cups cold water

Rinse the rice by pouring it into a heavy 2-quart saucepan, adding enough cold water to cover it completely and giving the rice a thorough stir. Drain the rice, add the 1¾ cups of fresh cold water and bring the rice to a boil over high heat. If you have any reason to think the rice you are using is old—and, therefore, very dry—add another ¼ cup of water. Boil for 2 to 3 minutes, or until craterlike holes appear in the surface of the rice. Then cover the pan tightly, reduce the heat to low and cook for 20 minutes. Turn off the heat but do not uncover the pan. Let the rice rest for 10 minutes. Now remove the cover and fluff the rice with chopsticks or a fork. Serve the rice at once while it is still hot. If the rice must wait, keep it in a covered heatproof serving bowl in a preheated 250° oven. To reheat any leftover rice, place it in a colander and set the colander into 1 inch of water boiling in a large pot. Cover the pot and steam for 5 to 10 minutes—depending on how much rice you have.

Cha-chiang-mien

炸 醬 麵

BOILED EGG NOODLES WITH MEAT SAUCE

To serve 4

GARNISHES
1 medium cucumber
1 tablespoon finely chopped garlic
3 scallions, including the green tops, cut in 2-inch lengths and finely shredded

3 tablespoons peanut oil, or flavorless vegetable oil
1 pound boneless pork shoulder, freshly ground

2 tablespoons Chinese rice wine, or pale dry sherry
1/4 cup brown-bean sauce
2 scallions, including the green tops, finely chopped
1 teaspoon sugar
1/2 cup chicken stock, fresh or canned
1 pound fresh Chinese egg noodles, or substitute other narrow egg noodles

PREPARE AHEAD: 1. With a small, sharp knife, peel the cucumber. Then cut it in half and scoop out the seeds by running the tip of a teaspoon down the center of each half. Now cut the cucumber into 1/8-inch slices, and cut the slices into strips 1/8-inch wide and 2 inches long.

2. Arrange the cucumber, garlic and scallions side by side on a small serving plate.

3. Have the garnishes, and the oil, pork, wine, bean sauce, scallions, sugar, chicken stock and noodles within easy reach.

TO COOK: Set a 12-inch wok or 10-inch skillet over high heat for 30 seconds. Pour in 2 tablespoons of the oil, swirl it about in the pan and heat for another 30 seconds, turning the heat down to moderate if the oil begins to smoke. Add the ground pork and stir-fry for 2 to 3 minutes, or until it browns lightly. Add the wine, brown-bean sauce, chopped scallions and sugar, mix well, and pour in the chicken stock. Bring to a boil and cook rapidly over moderate heat for 8 to 10 minutes, stirring constantly, until all the stock has evaporated. Turn off the heat and cover the wok or skillet to keep the meat sauce warm.

In a 3- to 4-quart heavy saucepan, bring 2 quarts of water to a boil over high heat. Drop in the noodles and boil them vigorously, uncovered, for 5 minutes, stirring occasionally with a large fork to prevent them from sticking. Drain the noodles through a colander.

Serve the noodles immediately in the following fashion: Place them on a large, deep, heated platter or in a deep serving bowl and toss them about quickly with the remaining 1 tablespoon of oil. Ladle the meat sauce into a serving bowl, and pass the sauce and the cucumber, garlic and scallion garnishes separately.

Huo-t'ui-tan-chao-fan

火腿蛋炒飯

HAM AND EGG FRIED RICE

To serve 3 to 4

½ cup shelled, fresh peas, or
    substitute thoroughly defrosted
    frozen peas
3 tablespoons peanut oil, or flavorless
    vegetable oil
2 eggs, lightly beaten
3 cups Chinese boiled rice, prepared

according to the directions on page 43
1 teaspoon salt
2 ounces boiled ham, sliced ¼ inch
    thick and cut into ¼-inch dice
    (about ½ cup)
1 scallion, including the green top,
    finely chopped

PREPARE AHEAD: 1. Blanch fresh peas by dropping them into 4 cups of boiling water and letting them boil uncovered for 5 to 10 minutes, or until tender. Then drain and run cold water over them to stop their cooking and set their color. Frozen peas need only be thoroughly defrosted.

2. Have the peas, oil, eggs, rice, salt, ham and scallions handy.

TO COOK: Set a 12-inch wok or 10-inch skillet over high heat for 30 seconds. Pour in 1 tablespoon of oil, swirl it about in the pan and immediately reduce the heat to moderate. Pour in the beaten eggs. They will form a film on the bottom of the pan almost at once. Immediately lift this film gently with a fork and push it to the back of the pan so that the still-liquid eggs can spread across the bottom of the pan to cook. As soon as the eggs are set, but before they become dry or begin to brown, transfer them to a small bowl and break them up with a fork. Pour the remaining 2 tablespoons of oil into the pan, swirl it around and heat it for 30 seconds. Add the rice and stir-fry for 2 to 3 minutes until all the grains are coated with oil. Add the salt, then the peas and ham, and stir-fry for 20 seconds. Return the eggs to the pan, add the scallions and cook only long enough to heat the eggs through. Serve at once.

Cha-shao-chao-mien

义燒炒麵

NOODLES WITH ROAST PORK AND CHINESE CABBAGE

4 dried Chinese mushrooms, 1 to 1½ inches in diameter

½ pound Chinese cabbage (celery cabbage or *bok choy*)

3 tablespoons peanut oil, or flavorless vegetable oil

½ cup whole canned bamboo shoots cut into 2-inch-long and ⅛-inch-wide shreds

½ pound roast pork, sliced ½ inch thick and cut into 2-inch-long and ⅛-inch-wide shreds (about 1½ cups), prepared according to recipe

on page 65

1 tablespoon soy sauce

1 teaspoon salt

½ cup chicken stock, fresh or canned

2 teaspoons cornstarch dissolved in 2 tablespoons cold chicken stock, fresh or canned, or cold water

½ pound fresh Chinese egg noodles, or substitute other narrow egg noodles

1 scallion, including the green top, cut into 2 inch lengths and finely shredded

PREPARE AHEAD: 1. In a small bowl, cover the mushrooms with ½ cup of warm water and let them soak for 30 minutes. Discard the water. Cut away and discard the mushroom stems; cut each cap into ⅛-inch strips.

2. With a cleaver or sharp knife, trim the top leaves of the cabbage and the root ends. Separate the stalks and wash them under cold water. Cut each stalk, leaves and all, into strips about 2 inches long by ¼ wide.

3. Have the mushrooms, cabbage, oil, bamboo shoots, pork, soy sauce, salt, stock, cornstarch mixture and shredded scallions within easy reach.

TO COOK: Preheat the oven to 375°. In a 4-quart saucepan, bring 2 quarts of water to a boil over high heat. Drop in the noodles, bring to a boil again, and cook for 5 minutes, stirring occasionally. Drain the noodles, transfer them to a shallow baking dish and stir in 1 tablespoon of oil. Bake the noodles for 7 or 8 minutes, or until lightly browned, then turn them over and bake 7 or 8 minutes longer to brown the other side.

Meanwhile, prepare the sauce. Set a 12-inch wok or 10-inch skillet over high heat for 30 seconds. Pour in 2 tablespoons of oil, swirl it about in the pan for 30 seconds, turning the heat down to moderate if the oil smokes. Add the cabbage, mushrooms and bamboo shoots, and stir-fry for 2 minutes. Add the soy sauce and salt, mix well, then add the roast pork and stir-fry for 1 minute. Pour in the stock and bring to a boil. Give the cornstarch mixture a stir to recombine it, add it to the pan, and cook, stirring until the sauce thickens and clears. Turn off the heat and cover the pan.

When the noodles are ready, serve them at once from the baking dish. Transfer the pork and cabbage mixture to a heated bowl and serve topped with the shredded scallions. As a main course, this will serve 2 to 4.

Hsia-jen-ch'ao mi-fên 蝦仁炒米粉

STIR-FRIED RICE STICK NOODLES WITH SHRIMP AND VEGETABLES

⅓ pound rice stick noodles
½ pound celery cabbage
1 pound uncooked shrimp (30-36 to the pound)
4 tablespoons peanut oil, or flavorless vegetable oil

1 tablespoon Chinese rice wine, or pale dry sherry
1½ teaspoons salt
½ teaspoon sugar
1 tablespoon soy sauce
½ cup chicken stock, fresh or canned

PREPARE AHEAD: 1. In a large bowl, cover the rice stick noodles with cold water. Soak for 5 minutes, then drain thoroughly in a colander.

2. With a cleaver or sharp knife, trim off any wilted top leaves of the cabbage and the root ends. Separate the stalks, wash them thoroughly and slice each stalk lengthwise into ⅛-inch-wide strips.

3. Shell the shrimp, and, with a small, sharp knife, make a shallow incision down the back and lift out the black or white intestinal vein. Wash the shrimp, dry with paper towels and cut each in half lengthwise.

4. Have the above ingredients, the oil, wine, salt, sugar, soy sauce and chicken stock within easy reach.

TO COOK: Set a 12-inch wok or 10-inch skillet over high heat for 30 seconds. Pour in 2 tablespoons of oil, swirl it about in the pan and heat for another 30 seconds, turning the heat down to moderate if the oil begins to smoke. Add the shrimp and stir-fry for 1 minute, or until they turn pink. Add ½ teaspoon salt and the wine, stir once or twice, then transfer the contents of the pan to a plate and set aside. Pour 2 more tablespoons of oil into the pan, heat it for 30 seconds and in it, stir-fry the cabbage for 2 minutes. Then add a teaspoon of salt, sugar and noodles, and cook, stirring, for 1 minute. Pour in the soy sauce and stock, and boil briskly for 3 minutes, or until the liquid has evaporated. Return the shrimp to the pan and, stirring constantly, cook for 30 seconds. Transfer the entire contents of the pan to a heated platter and serve at once. As a main course, this will serve 2 to 4.

Fish and Seafood

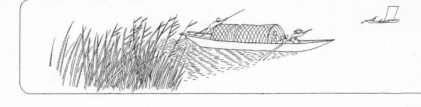

Tung-yü
JELLIED FISH

凍魚

A 1½-pound whiting, pike or sea bass, cleaned and with the head and tail removed (or substitute any other firm white fish)
1 tablespoon salt
2 tablespoons Chinese rice wine, or pale dry sherry

4 slices peeled fresh ginger root about 1 inch in diameter and ⅛ inch thick
1 scallion, including the green top, cut into 2-inch pieces
Fresh Chinese parsley sprigs (*cilantro*), or substitute flat-leaf Italian parsley

PREPARE AHEAD: 1. Wash the fish under cold running water and pat it dry with paper towels. To flavor and partially cure the fish, sprinkle it with salt, inside and out, and refrigerate for at least 4 hours.

TO COOK: Pour enough boiling water into the lower part of a steamer to come to within an inch of the cooking rack (or use a steamer substitute as described on page 8). Lay the fish on a deep heatproof platter ½ inch smaller than the diameter of the pot. Pour the wine over the fish, and scatter the ginger and scallions on top. Bring the water in the steamer to a rolling boil, place the fish on the rack and cover the pot. Keeping the water at a continuous boil, steam the fish for 15 minutes, or until it is quite firm to the touch. Remove the platter of fish from the steamer, discard the scallions and ginger, and, with a slotted spatula, transfer the fish to a cutting board or a large plate. Reserve the juices in the platter.

With a small, sharp knife, skin the fish by making a small slit at the base of the tail and peeling off the skin from tail to head. Carefully turn the fish over and skin the other side similarly. Now cut the top layer of the fish crosswise into 1-inch sections without cutting through the backbone. Detach them from the bone with the spatula and place the pieces of fish in a soup plate about 6 inches in diameter and 2 inches deep. Then lift out the backbone of the fish in one piece, discard it and divide the bottom layer of fish into similar portions. Pour the reserved juices over the fish and refrigerate for 4 hours, or until it jells. Garnish with fresh parsley. As part of a Chinese meal *(page 120)*, this will serve 4 to 6.

Hs'un-yü

熏 魚

SMOKED FISH

Despite its name, this fish is not smoked. In the traditional version of this recipe, the fish was smoked after it had been deep-fried, and the original name is still used for it.

A 2-pound carp or sea bass, cleaned and with head and tail removed (or use red snapper, pike, perch or other firm white fish)
1/4 cup soy sauce
1/4 cup Chinese rice wine, or pale dry sherry
1/2 teaspoon salt
4 slices peeled fresh ginger root,

about 1 inch in diameter and 1/8 inch thick
1 scallion, including the green top, cut into 2-inch lengths
1/4 cup chicken stock, fresh or canned
2 tablespoons dark brown sugar
3 cups peanut oil, or flavorless vegetable oil
1/2 teaspoon five-spice powder

PREPARE AHEAD: 1. Wash the fish quickly under cold running water, and pat it dry inside and out with paper towels. With a cleaver or heavy, sharp knife, split the fish in half by cutting along its backbone. Remove the bones, lay each half flat on a board and chop the halves crosswise into slices 1/2 inch wide.

2. In a large bowl, combine the soy sauce, wine, salt, ginger and scallions. Add the fish and toss it gently in the mixture to coat each strip thoroughly. Marinate at room temperature for 3 to 4 hours, stirring every hour or so.

3. Remove the fish slices from the marinade with a slotted spoon and drain them thoroughly on a rack. Strain the marinade through a sieve into a small saucepan, pressing down hard on the ginger and scallions to extract all their liquid before discarding them.

4. Have the fish marinade, oil, chicken stock, brown sugar and five-spice powder within easy reach.

TO COOK: Bring the pan of strained marinade to a boil over high heat, then reduce the heat to its lowest point, and stir in the chicken stock and brown sugar. Let the sauce simmer as slowly as possible while the fish is being fried.

Pour 3 cups of oil into a 12-inch wok or heavy deep-fryer and heat it until a haze forms above it or it registers 375° on a deep-frying thermometer. Drop the fish into the oil about 6 pieces at a time and deep-fry them for 5 minutes, or until they are crisp and a deep mahogany brown. Then pick them up one at a time with chopsticks or kitchen tongs, dip them in the simmering sauce and lay them side by side on a platter. Cool to room temperature. Just before serving, sprinkle the fish lightly with the five-spice powder. As a main course, smoked fish will serve 4 to 6. As part of a Chinese meal *(page 120)*, it will serve 6 to 8.

Hung-shao-yü

紅燒魚

RED-COOKED FISH

THE STUFFING

½ pound boneless lean pork, finely
  ground
1 tablespoon soy sauce
½ teaspoon cornstarch
½ teaspoon sugar
½ teaspoon salt
½ teaspoon finely chopped, peeled
  fresh ginger root

THE FISH

A 2-pound sea bass or carp, cleaned,
  but with head and tail left on (or
  substitute red snapper, pike, perch
  or any other firm white fish)
1 teaspoon salt
2 tablespoons flour

3 tablespoons peanut oil, or flavorless
  vegetable oil
¼ cup Chinese rice wine, or pale dry
  sherry
1 cup chicken stock, fresh or canned
5 tablespoons soy sauce
1 teaspoon sugar
2 scallions, including the green tops,
  cut into 2-inch lengths
4 slices peeled fresh ginger root,
  about 1 inch in diameter and ⅛
  inch thick
1 garlic clove, peeled and crushed
  with the side of the blade of a
  cleaver or heavy knife

PREPARE AHEAD: 1. For the stuffing, combine in a bowl the ground pork, soy sauce, cornstarch, sugar, salt and ginger, and, with a large spoon or your hands, mix them together thoroughly.

2. Wash the bass well under cold running water and pat it dry inside and out with paper towels. Place the fish flat on a chopping board and, with a cleaver or sharp, heavy knife, score the skin by making one row of diagonal cuts about 1 inch apart and ¼ to ½ inch deep across its length from head to tail. Then turn the fish over and score the other side. Sprinkle the fish inside and out with the salt.

3. Spread the flour over a sheet of wax paper and roll the fish about in it on both sides. Then lift the fish by the tail and shake off any excess flour.

4. Spoon the stuffing into the cavity of the fish and press the flaps firmly together to enclose the stuffing. (It is not necessary to sew or skewer the opening.)

5. Have the stuffed fish, oil, wine, chicken stock, soy sauce, scallions, ginger and garlic within easy reach.

TO COOK: Set a 12-inch wok or 12-inch skillet over high heat for 30 seconds. Pour in the 3 tablespoons of oil, swirl it about in the pan and heat for another 30 seconds, turning the heat down to moderate if the oil begins to smoke. Add the garlic, place the fish in the pan and let it brown for 5 minutes, regulating the heat under the pan to prevent the fish from burning. Then turn the fish over gently with a spatula or 2 large spoons and brown the other side. Now pour in the wine, chicken stock, soy sauce and sugar; scatter the scallions and ginger on top of the fish and cover the pan. Reduce the heat to moderate and cook the fish undisturbed for 15 minutes, adjusting the heat to keep the stock simmering. Baste the fish with the braising liquid, re-cover the pan and simmer for 15 minutes longer.

To serve, gently transfer the fish from the pan to a large heated platter. With a cleaver or sharp knife, cut the top layer of the fish into 1½-inch crosswise slices, but don't cut through the backbone. Remove and discard the ginger and garlic, then pour the braising sauce over the fish. Serve at once. When the top slices have been served, carefully remove the backbone and the little center bones attached to it. Then slice and serve the bottom layer of fish. As a main course, this will serve 4. As part of a Chinese meal *(page 120)*, it will serve 8 to 10.

Tou-shih-cheng-hsien-yü 豆豉蒸鮮魚
STEAMED SEA BASS WITH FERMENTED BLACK BEANS

A 1½-pound sea bass, cleaned but with head and tail left on (or substitute any other firm white fish)
1 teaspoon salt
2 teaspoons fermented black beans
1 tablespoon soy sauce
1 tablespoon Chinese rice wine, or pale dry sherry
1 tablespoon finely shredded, peeled fresh ginger root
1 scallion, including the green top, cut into 2-inch lengths
1 tablespoon peanut oil, or flavorless vegetable oil
½ teaspoon sugar

PREPARE AHEAD: 1. Wash the bass under cold running water and pat it dry inside and out with paper towels. With a sharp knife, lightly score the fish by making diagonal cuts ¼ inch deep at ½-inch intervals on both sides. Then sprinkle the fish, inside and out, with the salt.

2. With a cleaver or knife, coarsely chop the fermented beans, then combine them in a bowl with the soy sauce, wine, oil and sugar. Mix well.

3. Lay the fish on a heatproof platter ½ inch smaller in diameter than the pot you plan to steam it in. Pour the bowl of seasonings over the fish, and arrange the pieces of ginger and scallion on top.

TO COOK: Pour enough boiling water into the lower part of a steamer to come within an inch of the cooking rack (or use a steamer substitute as described on page 8). Bring the water in the steamer to a rolling boil and place the platter of fish on the rack. Cover the pot securely. Keep the water in the steamer at a continuous boil and replenish it if it boils away. Steam the fish for about 15 minutes, or until it is firm to the touch. Serve at once on its own steaming platter placed on top of a serving dish. As a main course, this will serve 3 or 4. As part of a Chinese meal *(page 120)*, it will serve 4 to 6.

Sung-shu-yü

松鼠魚

SQUIRREL FISH

This is called squirrel fish because the body curls as it is deep-fried—and, when arranged on a plate with the head, the fish is said to look like a squirrel. This recipe uses catsup as a substitute for Chinese crab-apple candy, which has a sweet-sour taste like catsup, but needs lengthy soaking.

To serve 4 to 6

2 dried Chinese mushrooms, 1 to 1½ inches in diameter'
¼ cup freshly shelled peas, or substitute thoroughly defrosted frozen peas
A 2-pound sea bass, cleaned, but with head and tail left on, or substitute pike, carp, red snapper or another firm white fish
3 cups plus 2 additional tablespoons peanut oil, or flavorless vegetable oil
½ cup flour
1 small onion, cut into ¼-inch-thick slices

1 small carrot, scraped and roll-cut into 1-inch wedges
4 peeled and washed fresh water chestnuts or drained canned water chestnuts, cut into ½-inch dice
1 teaspoon finely chopped garlic
1 teaspoon salt
¼ cup white vinegar
¼ cup sugar
1 teaspoon Chinese rice wine, or pale dry sherry
1 teaspoon soy sauce
2 tablespoons tomato catsup
½ cup chicken stock, fresh or canned
1 tablespoon cornstarch, dissolved in 2 tablespoons cold chicken stock, fresh or canned, or cold water

PREPARE AHEAD: 1. In a small bowl, cover the mushrooms with ½ cup of warm water and let them soak for 30 minutes. Discard the water. Cut away and discard the stems, and cut each cap into quarters.

2. Blanch the fresh peas and carrot wedges in a quart of boiling water for 7 to 10 minutes, or until tender. Drain, run cold water over them.

3. Wash the bass under cold running water and pat it dry inside and out with paper towels. With a cleaver or heavy, sharp knife, remove the head at the point where it joins the body. Turn the head upside down and, with a few sharp blows of a cleaver or heavy knife, break the head bone in the middle. Then, with the palm of your hand, press down firmly on the top of the head to flatten it. Lay the fish on its side and split it in half, cutting along the backbone, but do not remove the tail. Lift out the backbone, severing it at the base of the tail. Score the flesh side of each fillet with crisscrossing diagonal cuts an inch apart and almost down to the skin. The bass should be 2 separate fillets joined at the tail.

4. Have the above ingredients, oil, flour, onion, water chestnuts, garlic, salt, vinegar, sugar, wine, soy sauce, catsup, stock and cornstarch mixture at hand.

TO COOK: Preheat the oven to 250°. Pour 3 cups of oil into a 12-inch wok or a large deep-fryer and heat the oil until a haze forms above it or it reaches 375° on a deep-frying thermometer. Sprinkle the flour over a piece of wax paper and press the scored sides of the fish into it. Then coat the skin sides. Hold the fish by the tail, shake it to remove any excess flour and lower it into the hot oil. Flour the head and add it to the pan. Deep-fry the fish for 5 to 8 minutes until the body and head are golden brown. Lift the fish out of the oil and drain on a double thickness of paper towels. Place the fish, skin side down, on a heated platter and set the head in its original position. Keep the fish warm in the oven.

Set a 12-inch wok or 10-inch skillet over high heat for 30 seconds. Pour in 2 tablespoons of oil, swirl it about in the pan and heat for 30 seconds, turning the heat down if the oil smokes. Add the mushrooms, peas, carrot, onion, water chestnuts and garlic, and stir-fry for 3 minutes. Add the salt, then the vinegar, sugar, wine, soy sauce, catsup and stock, and bring to a boil. Stir the cornstarch mixture and add it. Cook, stirring, until the vegetables are glazed. Pour over the fish and serve at once.

Ch'ao-yü-pien
STIR-FRIED FISH FILLETS

炒魚片

1 pound boneless skinned sea bass
  or yellow pike fillets (or substitute
  any other firm white fish fillets)
2 teaspoons cornstarch
1 egg white
1 tablespoon Chinese rice wine, or
  pale dry sherry
2 teaspoons salt

4 tablespoons peanut oil, or flavorless
  vegetable oil
1 teaspoon finely chopped, peeled
  fresh ginger root
1 scallion, including the green top,
  finely chopped

PREPARE AHEAD: 1. Wash the fish fillets under cold running water and pat them dry with paper towels. With a cleaver or sharp knife, cut the fillets into 1½-inch squares about ½ inch thick.

2. Place the 2 teaspoons of cornstarch in a small bowl, add the fish pieces and toss them about until each piece is lightly coated. Add the egg white, wine and salt, and stir until thoroughly mixed.

3. Have the fish, and the oil, ginger slices and scallions within easy reach.

TO COOK: Set a 12-inch wok or 10-inch skillet over high heat for about 30 seconds. Pour in the 4 tablespoons of oil, swirl it about in the pan and heat for another 30 seconds, turning the heat down to moderate if the oil begins to smoke. Immediately add the ginger and scallions, and cook for a few seconds, but make sure they don't burn. Add the coated fish pieces and stir-fry gently for about 1 minute, or until the fish is firm and white. Transfer the entire contents of the pan to a heated platter and serve at once. As a main course, this will serve 2 to 4. As part of a Chinese meal *(page 120)*, it will serve 4 to 6.

Tou-shih-hsia-jen

STIR-FRIED SHRIMP WITH LOBSTER SAUCE

豆豉蝦仁

The somewhat confusing name for this dish does not mean, as you might think, that there is lobster in the sauce. It indicates that the shrimp is made with the same sauce used to prepare lobster Cantonese.

1 pound small raw shrimp in their shells (about 26 to 30 to the pound)
1/4 cup peanut oil, or flavorless vegetable oil
1 tablespoon Chinese rice wine, or pale dry sherry
2 teaspoons fermented black beans, chopped
1 teaspoon finely chopped garlic
1/4 pound lean pork, freshly ground
1 tablespoon soy sauce

1 teaspoon salt
1/4 teaspoon sugar
1/8 teaspoon freshly ground black pepper
1 scallion, including the green top, finely chopped
1 cup chicken stock, fresh or canned
2 tablespoons cornstarch dissolved in 3 tablespoons cold chicken stock, fresh or canned, or cold water
2 eggs, lightly beaten

PREPARE AHEAD: 1. Shell the shrimp but leave the tail shell attached. With a small, sharp knife, devein the shrimp by making a shallow incision down their backs and lifting out the black or white intestinal veins with the point of the knife. Wash the shrimp under cold running water, pat them dry with paper towels and put them aside.

2. Have the shrimp, oil, wine, pork, garlic, black beans, salt, soy sauce, sugar, pepper, scallions, chicken stock, cornstarch mixture and beaten eggs within easy reach.

TO COOK: Set a 12-inch wok or 10-inch skillet over high heat for 30 seconds. Pour in 2 tablespoons of the oil, swirl it about in the pan and heat for another 30 seconds, turning down the heat to moderate if the oil begins to smoke. Drop in the shrimp and stir-fry for about 1 minute, or until the shrimp turn pink. Stir in the wine, then remove the shrimp mixture to a plate. Add the remaining 2 tablespoons of oil to the pan. Add the fermented black beans and garlic, and stir for a few seconds, making sure the garlic doesn't burn. Add the pork and stir-fry for 2 or 3 minutes until the meat is no longer pink. Stir in the soy sauce, salt, sugar, pepper, scallions and reserved shrimp, then pour in the chicken stock. Cover the pan and bring the stock to a boil. Give the cornstarch mixture a quick stir to recombine it and add it to the pan. When the sauce has thickened and become clear—about 30 seconds—pour in the beaten eggs in a slow stream, meanwhile, with a large spoon, lifting the contents of the pan gently from the sides so that the eggs merge with all the ingredients without any further cooking. Transfer the entire contents of the pan to a heated platter and serve at once. As a main course, this will serve 2 to 4. As part of a Chinese meal *(page 120),* it will serve 4 to 6.

Ch'ao-hsia-jen
炒蝦仁

STIR-FRIED SHRIMP WITH PEAS

1 pound raw shrimp in their shells
(about 26 to 30 to the pound)
1 pound fresh peas, shelled, or 1 cup
thoroughly defrosted frozen peas
2 teaspoons cornstarch
1 egg white
2 teaspoons Chinese rice wine, or pale
dry sherry

1 teaspoon salt
3 tablespoons peanut oil, or
flavorless vegetable oil
1 scallion, including the green top,
cut into 2-inch lengths
3 slices peeled fresh ginger root,
about 1 inch in diameter and ⅛
inch thick

PREPARE AHEAD: 1. Shell the shrimp and, with a small, sharp knife, devein them by making a shallow incision down the back and lifting out the black or white intestinal vein with the point of the knife. Wash the shrimp under cold running water and pat them thoroughly dry with paper towels. Split each shrimp in half lengthwise, then cut each of the halves in two, crosswise.

2. Blanch the freshly shelled peas by dropping them into a quart of rapidly boiling water and letting them boil uncovered for 5 to 7 minutes, or until just tender when tasted. Then drain the peas into a large sieve or colander, and run cold water over them for a few seconds to stop their cooking and set their color. The frozen peas need only be thoroughly defrosted.

3. In a large mixing bowl, combine the shrimp and cornstarch, and toss them together with a spoon until each shrimp piece is lightly coated with cornstarch. Add the egg white, wine and salt, and stir them with the shrimp until they are thoroughly mixed together. Set the mixture aside for at least one hour.

4. Have the shrimp, peas, oil, scallions and ginger within easy reach.

TO COOK: Set a 12-inch wok or 10-inch skillet over high heat for 30 seconds. Pour in the 3 tablespoons of oil, swirl it about in the pan and heat for another 30 seconds, turning the heat down to moderate if the oil begins to smoke. Add the scallions and ginger, and stir-fry for 30 seconds to flavor the oil, then remove them with a slotted spoon and discard. Immediately drop the shrimp into the pan and stir-fry them for 2 minutes, or until they turn pink. Do not let the shrimp overcook. Then drop in the peas and stir-fry for about 1 minute to heat the peas through. Transfer the entire contents of the pan to a heated platter and serve at once. As a main course, this will serve 2 to 4. As part of a Chinese meal *(page 120)*, it will serve 4 to 6.

Hsien-kan-pei-yao-hua

鮮干貝腰花

STIR-FRIED SEA SCALLOPS AND PORK KIDNEYS

4 pork kidneys
½ pound fresh or thoroughly
   defrosted frozen sea scallops
¼ cup peanut oil, or flavorless
   vegetable oil
1 tablespoon Chinese rice wine, or
   pale dry sherry
1 teaspoon finely chopped, peeled
   fresh ginger root

1 scallion, including the green top,
   finely chopped
2 tablespoons soy sauce
½ teaspoon salt
1 teaspoon sugar
1 teaspoon cornstarch dissolved in 1
   tablespoon chicken stock, fresh or
   canned, or cold water

PREPARE AHEAD: 1. Peel off the thin outer membrane covering the kidneys, if the butcher has not already removed it, with a cleaver or sharp knife. Split the kidneys in half lengthwise and cut away the small knobs of fat and any tough membrane surrounding them. Place the kidney halves flat side down on a chopping board and score their surfaces diagonally to create a crisscross pattern, cutting about two thirds of the way down into them and spacing the cuts about ¼ inch apart. Then cut the kidneys crosswise into 1-inch slices, and cut the slices into strips about 2 inches long.

2. Wash the scallops under cold running water, pat them dry with paper towels and cut them horizontally into slices ¼ inch thick.

3. Have the above ingredients, and the oil, wine, ginger, scallions, soy sauce, salt, sugar and the cornstarch mixture within easy reach.

TO COOK: Set a 12-inch wok or 10-inch skillet over high heat for 30 seconds. Pour in 2 tablespoons of oil, swirl it about in the pan and heat for another 30 seconds, turning the heat down to moderate if the oil begins to smoke. Add the scallops and stir-fry for only 1 minute, or until they turn white but not too firm. Immediately pour in the wine and add the salt, stir well, and, with a large spoon, transfer the scallops to a plate. Pour the remaining 2 tablespoons of oil into the pan, heat for about 30 seconds, and add the ginger and scallions. Stir for a few seconds and drop in the kidneys. Stir-fry over high heat for 2 minutes, or until their edges begin to curl. Then add the soy sauce and sugar. Return the scallops and their accumulated juices to the pan, and mix with the kidneys for a few seconds. Give the cornstarch mixture a quick stir to recombine it and add it to the pan. When the kidneys and scallops are coated with a light, clear glaze—this will take no more than a few seconds—transfer the entire contents of the pan to a heated platter and serve at once. As a main course this will serve 4. As part of a Chinese meal (page 120), it will serve 6 to 8.

Cha-hsia-ch'iu 炸蝦球

DEEP-FRIED SHRIMP BALLS

To make about 2 dozen

1 slice fresh white bread
2 tablespoons cold chicken stock,
  fresh or canned, or cold water
1 pound uncooked shrimp in their
  shells
2 ounces fresh pork fat (¼ cup)
4 peeled and washed fresh water
  chestnuts, finely chopped, or 4
  drained canned water chestnuts,

finely chopped
1 teaspoon salt
½ teaspoon finely chopped, peeled
  fresh ginger root
1 egg yolk
1 egg white
3 cups peanut oil, or flavorless
  vegetable oil
Roasted salt and pepper, prepared
  according to the recipe on page 93

PREPARE AHEAD: 1. Trim crust from the bread and tear bread into small pieces. Place them in a bowl and sprinkle with the stock or water.

2. Shell the shrimp. With a small, sharp knife, make a shallow incision down their backs and lift out the intestinal vein with the point of the knife. Wash the shrimp under cold water and pat them dry with paper towels. With a cleaver or sharp knife, chop the shrimp and pork fat together until they form a smooth paste.

3. In a bowl, combine the soaked bread, shrimp mixture, water chestnuts, salt, ginger and egg yolk, and mix thoroughly. Beat the egg white to a froth with a fork or whisk, and stir it into the shrimp mixture.

4. Have the shrimp mixture, a bowl of cold water, a baking pan lined with a double thickness of paper towels, and the oil within easy reach.

TO COOK: Preheat the oven to its lowest setting. Pour 3 cups of oil into a 12-inch wok or large deep-fat fryer and heat until a haze forms above it or it reaches 350° on a deep-frying thermometer. Take a handful of the shrimp mixture and squeeze your fingers into a fist, forcing the mixture up between your thumb and forefinger. When it forms a ball about the size of a walnut, use a spoon to scoop off the ball and drop it in the hot oil. Repeat until you have made 6 to 8 balls, dipping the spoon into the bowl of cold water each time to prevent sticking. Turn them with a Chinese strainer or slotted spoon to keep the balls apart as they fry. They should become golden in 2 to 3 minutes. Transfer the fried balls to the paper-lined baking pan to drain and keep warm in the oven while you fry the rest. Transfer the finished shrimp balls to a heated platter and serve with roasted salt and pepper dip *(page 93)*. As an hors d'oeuvre or part of a Chinese meal *(page 120)*, this will serve 6 to 8.

Fêng-wei-hsia

鳳尾蝦

DEEP-FRIED PHOENIX-TAILED SHRIMP

1 pound raw shrimp in their shells
(about 28 to 30 to the pound)
1 tablespoon Chinese rice wine, or
pale dry sherry
1 teaspoon salt
⅛ teaspoon ground white pepper

THE BATTER
1½ cups sifted flour

1 cup cold water
1 tablespoon double-acting baking
powder

4 cups peanut oil or flavorless
vegetable oil
Roasted salt and pepper, prepared
according to the recipe on page
93

PREPARE AHEAD: 1. Peel off each shrimp shell down to the last section, leaving it and the tail attached to the shrimp. Cut down the back of each shrimp with a small, sharp knife and remove the black or white intestinal vein. Wash the shrimp under cold running water and pat them dry with paper towels. Cut the shrimp ¾ of the way through along their inner curves and flatten them with the side of a cleaver or large, heavy knife. Combine the wine, salt and pepper. Spread the shrimp out flat and sprinkle the cut side of each one with the mixture.

2. To make the batter, pour the flour into a bowl, gradually stir in the water to form a smooth paste, then add the baking powder.

3. Have the shrimp and oil within easy reach. Preheat the oven to 250° and place in it a shallow baking dish lined with a double thickness of paper towels.

TO COOK: Pour the oil into a 12-inch wok or heavy deep-fryer and heat it until a haze forms above it or it registers 375° on a deep-frying thermometer. Pick up the shrimp by their tails, dip one at a time into the batter and then drop them carefully into the hot oil. Fry only 6 at a time, turning them once or twice, for 2 or 3 minutes, or until golden brown. Drain them in the paper-lined dish and keep them warm in the oven while you deep-fry the remaining shrimp. Serve on a heated platter, accompanied by the roasted salt and pepper. As a main course, this will serve 2 to 4. As part of a Chinese meal *(page 120),* it will serve 4 to 6.

Kan-shao-hsia-jen

乾燒蝦仁

STIR-FRIED SHRIMP WITH PEPPER SAUCE

1 pound fresh shrimp in their shells
  (about 26 to 30 to the pound)
1 tablespoon finely chopped, peeled
  fresh ginger root
1 teaspoon coarsely chopped garlic
4 scallions, including the green tops,
  cut into ¼-inch pieces
1 tablespoon Chinese rice wine, or
  pale dry sherry
2 tablespoons soy sauce

1 teaspoon sugar
½ teaspoon salt
½ teaspoon crushed red-pepper
  flakes
2 tablespoons tomato catsup
1 tablespoon cornstarch dissolved in
  2 tablespoons cold chicken stock,
  fresh or canned, or cold water
2 tablespoons peanut oil, or flavorless
  vegetable oil

PREPARE AHEAD: 1. Shell and devein the shrimp. Then wash them under cold running water, drain and pat them dry with paper towels. Refrigerate until ready to use.

2. Have the shrimp, and the oil, ginger, garlic, scallions, red-pepper flakes, wine, soy sauce, tomato catsup, sugar, salt and cornstarch mixture within easy reach.

TO COOK: Set a 12-inch wok or 10-inch skillet over high heat for about 30 seconds. Pour in 2 tablespoons of oil, swirl it about in the pan and heat for another 30 seconds, reducing the heat to moderate if the oil begins to smoke. Immediately add the chopped ginger, garlic, scallions and red-pepper flakes, stir-fry for about 20 seconds, and drop in the shrimp. Cook, stirring constantly, for 1 or 2 minutes, or until the shrimp turn pink and firm. Add the wine, soy sauce and tomato catsup, sugar and salt; stir once or twice. Give the cornstarch mixture a quick stir to recombine it and add it to the pan, stirring continuously, until the mixture thickens and coats the shrimp with a translucent glaze. Transfer to a heated platter and serve at once. As a main course, this will serve 4. As part of a Chinese meal *(page 120)*, it will serve 6 to 8.

Hsieh-jou-pan-huang-kua
蟹肉拌黄瓜
CRABMEAT AND CUCUMBER SALAD

2 medium-sized cucumbers
½ pound fresh crabmeat or one
    7½-ounce can crabmeat
2 tablespoons white vinegar

2 tablespoons soy sauce
1 teaspoon sugar
⅛ teaspoon ground white pepper
1 tablespoon sesame-seed oil

PREPARE AHEAD: 1. Pick over the crabmeat and discard all bits of shell and cartilage.

2. Peel the cucumbers and cut them lengthwise in two. With a small spoon, scrape the seeds out of each half, leaving hollow, boatlike shells. Shred the cucumbers, not too fine, with a cleaver or large, sharp knife.

TO ASSEMBLE: In a small glass or porcelain bowl, combine the vinegar, soy sauce, sugar, pepper and sesame-seed oil, and mix well. Add the cucumbers and crabmeat; toss to coat thoroughly with the dressing and chill slightly—no more than an hour—before serving. As a salad course, this will serve 4 to 6. As a cold dish at a Chinese meal *(page 120)*, it will serve 6 to 8.

Pao-yü-ts'ai-hsin
鮑魚菜心
STIR-FRIED ABALONE WITH CHINESE CABBAGE

To serve 4 to 6

1 pound Chinese cabbage, celery
    cabbage or *bok choy*
½ cup ⅛-inch slices canned abalone,
    preferably Mexican abalone
2 tablespoons peanut oil, or flavorless
    vegetable oil

1 teaspoon salt
¼ cup abalone juice, or fresh or
    canned chicken stock
1 teaspoon cornstarch dissolved in 1
    tablespoon abalone juice, or cold
    chicken stock, fresh or canned, or
    cold water

PREPARE AHEAD: 1. With a cleaver or sharp knife, trim off the top wilted leaves and root ends of the cabbage. Separate the stalks and wash them thoroughly under cold running water. Cut each stalk, leaves and all, into 2-by-½-inch pieces.

2. Have the cabbage, and the abalone, oil, salt, abalone juice (or chicken stock) and cornstarch mixture within easy reach.

TO COOK: Set a 12-inch wok or 10-inch skillet over moderate heat for about 30 seconds. Pour in the 2 tablespoons of oil, swirl it about in the pan and heat again for 30 seconds, turning the heat down to moderate if the oil begins to smoke. Add the cabbage. Stir-fry for about 1 minute to coat the cabbage thoroughly with the oil, then add the salt and abalone juice or chicken stock. Bring to a quick boil, cover the pan and cook over moderate heat for about 3 minutes. Stir in the abalone and immediately give the cornstarch mixture a quick stir to recombine it and add it to the pan. As soon as the cabbage and abalone are coated with a light, clear glaze, transfer the entire contents of the pan to a heated platter and serve at once.

Hsieh-jou-tou fu

蟹肉豆腐

STIR-FRIED CRABMEAT WITH BEAN CURD

½ pound fresh crabmeat or one 7½ ounce can of crabmeat

4 three-inch squares fresh bean curd, about ½ inch thick

3 tablespoons peanut oil, or flavorless vegetable oil

1 scallion, including the green top, finely chopped

1 teaspoon finely chopped, peeled fresh ginger root

1½ teaspoons salt

¼ cup chicken stock, fresh or canned

⅛ teaspoon ground black pepper

2 teaspoons cornstarch dissolved in 2 tablespoons chicken stock, fresh or canned, or cold water

PREPARE AHEAD: 1. Pick over the crabmeat, and discard all bits of shell and cartilage.

2. Slice each square of bean curd into ¼-inch slices, and cut the slices in half to make 24 strips 1½ inches long and 1 inch wide.

3. Have the above ingredients, and the oil, scallions, ginger, salt, stock, black pepper and cornstarch mixture within easy reach.

TO COOK: Set a 12-inch wok or 10-inch skillet over high heat for 30 seconds. Pour in the oil, swirl it about in the pan and heat for another 30 seconds, turning the heat down to moderate if the oil begins to smoke. Add the scallions and ginger, stir once or twice, then add the bean curd, salt and chicken stock. Bring to a boil, cover the pan and cook over moderate heat for 2 or 3 minutes. Gently stir in the crabmeat and black pepper, and heat through for about 1 minute. Give the cornstarch mixture a quick stir to recombine it and pour it over the crabmeat. Cook for another minute, stirring constantly, until the crabmeat and bean curd are coated with a light, clear glaze. Transfer to a platter and serve at once. As a main course, this will serve 4. As part of a Chinese meal (page 120), it will serve 6 to 8.

Ch'ao-lung-hsia
LOBSTER CANTONESE

炒龍蝦

1 live lobster, 1¼ to 1½ pounds
2 tablespoons peanut oil, or flavorless vegetable oil
2 teaspoons fermented black beans, chopped
1 teaspoon finely chopped garlic
¼ pound lean boneless pork, finely ground
1 teaspoon soy sauce

1 teaspoon salt
¼ teaspoon sugar
⅛ teaspoon white pepper
1 scallion, including the green top, finely chopped
1 cup chicken stock, fresh or canned
2 tablespoons cornstarch dissolved in 3 tablespoons cold water
2 eggs, lightly beaten

PREPARE AHEAD: 1. Lay the lobster, shell side up, on a chopping board. Wrap one hand in a towel and hold the lobster firmly in place. With a cleaver or large, heavy knife, chop off the head at the first joint in the shell. Twist off the large claws at the point where they are joined to the body. Then separate the claws themselves from the joints, and chop both claws and joints in two lengthwise. Chop off and discard the small joints of the legs, leaving only the joint that had been nearest the body. Cut off and discard the antennae and eyes, and pull the outer shell off the head of the lobster. Save the inner cartilagelike shell but remove the gelatinous stomach sac and the gills. Now turn the lobster over, and split the body and tail in half lengthwise. Save the brownish-green tomalley (or liver) and the black coral (or roe) if there is any, but discard the long, white intestinal vein. Then, cutting crosswise, chop the body and the tail into 1-inch pieces.

2. Have the lobster, and the oil, chopped black beans, garlic, pork, soy sauce, salt, sugar, pepper, scallions, chicken stock, cornstarch mixture and beaten eggs within easy reach.

TO COOK: Set a 12-inch wok or 10-inch skillet over high heat for about 30 seconds. Pour in the oil, swirl it about in the pan and heat for another 30 seconds, then turn down the heat to moderate. Add the fermented black beans and garlic, and stir for a few seconds, making sure the garlic doesn't burn. Add the pork and stir-fry for 1 minute until the meat is no longer pink. Stir in the soy sauce, salt, sugar, pepper and scallions. When all the ingredients are well combined, add the lobster pieces and stir-fry over high heat for about 1 minute. Pour in the chicken stock, cover and cook undisturbed for 5 minutes. Give the cornstarch mixture a quick stir to recombine it and pour it into the pan. When the sauce has thickened and become clear, pour in the beaten eggs in a slow stream, gently lifting the contents of the pan from the sides with a spoon or fork as you pour. Immediately turn off the heat and transfer the entire contents of the pan to a large heated platter. Serve at once. As a main course, this will serve 2 to 4. As part of a Chinese meal *(page 120)*, it will serve 4 to 6.

Meat

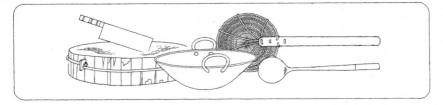

Tou-sh'ih-pai-ku

豆豉排骨

BRAISED SPARERIBS WITH FERMENTED BLACK BEANS

1 pound lean spareribs
1 large clove garlic, crushed and
    peeled
1 tablespoon peanut oil, or flavorless
    vegetable oil
1 tablespoon soy sauce
1 teaspoon sugar

1 tablespoon fermented black beans,
    chopped
½ cup cold water
1 teaspoon cornstarch dissolved in 1
    tablespoon cold chicken stock,
    fresh or canned, or cold water

PREPARE AHEAD: 1. With a cleaver or large, sharp knife, separate the spareribs and chop them crosswise into 1½-inch lengths.

2. Have the spareribs, and the oil, soy sauce, sugar, fermented black beans and ½ cup of water within easy reach.

TO COOK: Set a 12-inch wok or 10-inch skillet over high heat for 30 seconds. Pour in the oil, swirl it about in the pan and heat for another 30 seconds, turning the heat down if the oil begins to smoke. Add the spareribs and stir-fry them for 3 to 4 minutes until they are lightly browned on both sides. Add the garlic, soy sauce, sugar, black beans and water, and stir to coat the spareribs. Bring to a boil, cover the pan and reduce the heat to low. Simmer for about an hour, turning the spareribs occasionally.

To serve, arrange the spareribs on a heated platter. Skim and discard the surface fat from the sauce and remove the garlic. Give the cornstarch mixture a quick stir to recombine it and pour it into the pan. Cook, stirring, for a few seconds until the sauce thickens and clears. Then pour it over the ribs and serve at once. As a main course, this will serve 2. As part of a Chinese meal *(page 120)*, it will serve 4 to 6.

Shih-tzŭ-tou

獅子頭

LION'S HEAD

Because the large pork balls are said to suggest the heads of lions and the cabbage served with them their manes, this dish is fancifully known as "lion's head."

1 pound boneless pork, finely ground
3 tablespoons soy sauce
1 tablespoon Chinese rice wine, or
    pale dry sherry
1 scallion, including the green top,
    finely chopped
1 teaspoon finely chopped, peeled
    fresh ginger root
4 water chestnuts, finely chopped
1 egg, lightly beaten

3 tablespoons cornstarch dissolved in
    2 tablespoons chicken stock, fresh
    or canned, or cold water
1 pound Chinese cabbage (celery
    cabbage or *bok choy*)
2 tablespoons peanut oil, or flavorless
    vegetable oil
½ teaspoon sugar
½ cup chicken stock, fresh or canned

PREPARE AHEAD: 1. With a large spoon or your hands, mix together thoroughly the pork, 2 tablespoons of the soy sauce, wine, scallion, ginger, water chestnuts, egg and 1 tablespoon of the cornstarch mixture. Shape the meat mixture lightly into 4 to 6 balls. Set aside.

2. With a cleaver or sharp knife, trim the wilted ends from the cabbage and cut off the root end. Separate the stalks and wash under cold running water. Cut each stalk in two lengthwise, then slice the pieces crosswise at 3-inch intervals.

3. Have the above ingredients, and the remaining cornstarch mixture and soy sauce, the oil, sugar and stock within easy reach.

TO COOK: Arrange half the cabbage in a layer on the bottom of a 2- to 3-quart heavy flameproof casserole. Set a 10-inch skillet over high heat for about 30 seconds. Pour in 2 tablespoons of oil, swirl it about in the pan and heat for another 30 seconds, turning the heat down to moderate if the oil begins to smoke. Give the cornstarch mixture a quick stir to recombine it. One at a time, dip the meatballs into the cornstarch, coating them thoroughly, and put them at once into the skillet. Fry the meatballs, turning them only once with a large spoon, for 2 minutes, or until they are golden brown on both sides. Gently remove them from the pan and place them on the bed of cabbage. Arrange the remaining cabbage over them. Mix the sugar, the remaining tablespoon of soy sauce and ½ cup of chicken stock together and pour it into the casserole. Bring to a boil over high heat, then cover the casserole tightly, reduce the heat to its lowest point and simmer for about an hour. Check after about a half hour to make certain all the liquid hasn't cooked away. If it has, add ¼ cup of chicken stock or water. Serve from the casserole or arrange the cabbage mixture on a heated platter with the meatballs on top and pour the pan juices over them. Lion's head will serve 4 to 6, depending on the number of pork balls.

Ch'a-shao 义燒

ROAST PORK STRIPS

2 pounds boneless pork, preferably
    butt
2 tablespoons chicken stock, fresh or
    canned
2 tablespoons soy sauce
1 tablespoon brown-bean sauce,
    mashed

1 tablespoon Chinese rice wine, or
    pale dry sherry
1½ tablespoons sugar
¾ teaspoon salt
1 teaspoon finely chopped garlic
2 to 3 drops red food coloring

PREPARE AHEAD: 1. With a cleaver or a large, sharp knife, cut the pork butt into 1½- to 2-inch-wide strips. Lay the strips flat and cut them in half lengthwise. Depending on the original size of the butt, you should have from 6 to 8 long, thick strips. Lay the strips flat in one or two layers in a large, shallow dish or pan long enough to hold them easily.

2. In a small bowl, combine the chicken stock, soy sauce, brown-bean sauce, wine, sugar, salt, garlic and food coloring. Stir until the ingredients are well mixed. Pour the sauce over the pork strips, baste them thoroughly and let them marinate for at least 3 hours at room temperature or for at least 6 hours in the refrigerator. Turn the strips over in the marinade every hour or so.

TO COOK: Preheat the oven to 350°. To catch the drippings of the pork strips as they roast and to prevent the oven from smoking as well, fill a large, shallow roasting pan with water and place it on the lowest rack of the oven. Insert one curved tip of an S-shaped hook at the end of each strip of pork. (Any hook will do: a curtain hook, S-hook, even a 5- or 6-inch length of heavy-duty wire or unpainted wire coat hanger bent into that shape.) Hang the hooks from the uppermost rack of the oven, directly above the pan of water. Roast the pork undisturbed for 45 minutes. Then increase the oven heat to 450° and roast for 15 minutes longer, or until the pork strips are crisp and a rich, golden brown. Remove the pork from the oven, take out the hooks and cut the strips crosswise into paper-thin slices. Serve the sliced pork hot, arranged in overlapping layers, on a heated platter. As a main course, this will serve 4 to 6. As part of a Chinese meal *(page 120)*, it will serve 8 to 10.

If you like, the pork may be cooled to room temperature, or wrapped in aluminum foil and chilled in the refrigerator, and then presented as a cold meat course or as part of a Chinese cold plate. Leftover roast pork can be wrapped tightly and stored in the refrigerator or freezer for use in such recipes as steamed buns with pork filling *(page 10)* or ten-varieties hot pot *(page 30)*.

Mu-hsü-jou 木樨肉

SOFT-FRIED SHREDDED PORK AND EGGS

½ cup dried tiger lily buds (about 30 large buds)
¼ cup dried cloud ears
½ pound boneless pork shoulder
1 tablespoon Chinese rice wine, or pale dry sherry
1 tablespoon soy sauce
1 teaspoon cornstarch
1 teaspoon sugar

4 tablespoons peanut oil, or flavorless vegetable oil
4 eggs, lightly beaten
1 teaspoon salt
4 whole scallions, shredded
1 teaspoon sesame-seed oil
Mandarin pancakes, prepared according to the recipe on page 99 and reheated

PREPARE AHEAD: 1. In a small bowl, cover the tiger lily buds with 1 cup of warm water and let them soak for 30 minutes. Discard the water. Snap off and discard the hard ends of the buds, wash the buds in a colander under cold running water, drain, and cut each bud in half.

2. In another small bowl, cover the cloud ears with 1 cup of warm water and let them soak for 30 minutes. Discard the water. Wash the ears under cold running water, then break them into small pieces.

3. Place the pork on a chopping board and, holding the meat firmly, cut it horizontally into paper-thin slices with a cleaver or sharp knife. Then cut the slices into shreds 1½ to 2 inches long and ⅛ inch wide. Combine the wine, soy sauce, cornstarch and sugar in a bowl, add the pork shreds, and mix well.

4. Have the above ingredients, and the oil, lightly beaten eggs, salt and scallions within easy reach. Reheat the mandarin pancakes and keep them warm.

TO COOK: Set a 12-inch wok or 10-inch skillet over high heat for about 30 seconds. Pour in 2 tablespoons of oil, swirl it about in the pan and immediately reduce the heat to moderate. Pour in the beaten eggs. They will form a film on the bottom of the pan almost at once. Immediately push it to the back of the pan with a fork so that the still-liquid eggs on top can spread into the bottom of the pan to cook. As soon as the eggs are set and dry, but before they begin to brown, transfer them to a small bowl and break them up with a fork.

Pour 2 more tablespoons of oil into the pan, swirl it about and heat it for 30 seconds. Add the shredded pork mixture and stir-fry for 5 to 6 minutes until the meat loses its pink color. Add the tiger lily buds and cloud ears, and stir-fry for 1 minute, then add the scallions and salt, mix well, and stir in the scrambled eggs. Stir and cook for 1 minute longer, add the sesame-seed oil and serve at once in a deep platter, accompanied by the warm mandarin pancakes.

Traditionally, each guest spreads a pancake flat on his plate and places about 2 tablespoons of the pork mixture along the center of the pancake. The pancake is folded in half over the pork and tucked under it, one end of the package is then folded over about 1 inch to enclose the filling securely, and the whole rolled into a neat cylinder that can be picked up with the fingers and eaten. As a main course, this will serve 4. As part of a Chinese meal *(page 120)*, it will serve 6 to 8.

Fu-chu-jou-pien 腐 竹 肉 片
BRAISED PORK WITH BEAN CURD SKIN AND CHINESE MUSHROOMS

4 dried Chinese mushrooms, 1 to 1½ inches in diameter
¼ pound bean curd skin
1 pound lean, boneless pork
2 tablespoons soy sauce

½ teaspoon sugar
2 teaspoons cornstarch
3 tablespoons peanut oil, or flavorless vegetable oil
1 teaspoon salt

PREPARE AHEAD: 1. In a small bowl, cover the mushrooms with ½ cup of warm water and let them soak for 30 minutes. Remove them with a slotted spoon. Strain the water through a fine sieve and reserve ¼ cup of it. With a cleaver or sharp knife, cut away and discard the tough stems of the mushrooms, and cut each cap into quarters.

2. In a small bowl, cover the bean curd skin with 2 cups of boiling water and let it soak for 30 minutes. Then drain it, and cut it into strips 1 inch wide and 2 inches long.

3. With a cleaver or sharp knife, trim and discard any fat from the pork. Holding the meat flat on a chopping block, cut it against the grain into slices ⅛ inch thick. Then cut the slices into strips 1 inch wide and 2 inches long.

4. In a large bowl, combine the soy sauce, sugar and cornstarch, and mix them together thoroughly. Add the pork strips and toss them about with a spoon to coat them with the mixture.

5. Have the above ingredients, and the oil and salt within easy reach.

TO COOK: Set a 12-inch wok or 10-inch skillet over high heat for 30 seconds. Pour in the 3 tablespoons of oil, swirl it about in the pan and heat for another 30 seconds, turning the heat down to moderate if the oil begins to smoke. Add the pork and stir-fry for about 1 minute, or until the meat loses its reddish color. Drop in the bean curd skin, mushrooms and salt, and stir them about for a few seconds before pouring in the ¼ cup of reserved mushroom-soaking water. Bring to a boil, cover the pan and turn the heat down to low. Simmer undisturbed for 5 minutes, then transfer the entire contents of the pan to a heated platter and serve at once. As a main course, this serves 2 to 4. As part of a Chinese meal *(page 120)*, it will serve 4 to 6.

T'ien-suan-ku-lao-jou

甜酸古老肉

SWEET-AND-SOUR PORK

1 pound lean boneless pork,
  preferably butt
1 egg, lightly beaten
1 teaspoon salt
¼ cup cornstarch
¼ cup flour
¼ cup chicken stock, fresh or canned
3 cups peanut oil, or flavorless
  vegetable oil

SAUCE
1 tablespoon peanut oil, or flavorless
  vegetable oil

1 teaspoon finely chopped garlic
1 large green pepper, seeded, deribbed
  and cut into ½ inch squares
1 medium carrot, scraped and sliced
  into 2-inch strips ¼ inch wide and
  ¼ inch thick
½ cup chicken stock, fresh or canned
4 tablespoons sugar
4 tablespoons red-wine vinegar
1 teaspoon soy sauce
1 tablespoon cornstarch dissolved in
  2 tablespoons cold water

PREPARE AHEAD: 1. Trim the pork of any excess fat and, with a cleaver or sharp knife, cut the meat into 1-inch cubes.

2. In a large bowl, mix together the egg, ¼ cup cornstarch, ¼ cup flour, ¼ cup chicken stock and salt. Set aside.

3. For the sauce, have the oil, garlic, green pepper, carrot, chicken stock, sugar, vinegar, soy sauce and cornstarch mixture within easy reach.

TO COOK: Just before cooking, add the pork cubes to the egg and flour mixture, and stir until each piece of meat is well coated. Preheat the oven to 250°. Pour the 3 cups of oil into a wok and set it over high heat. When the oil almost begins to smoke or reaches 375° on a deep-frying thermometer, drop in half of the coated pork cubes one by one. Fry for 5 to 6 minutes, regulating the heat so that the pork turns a crisp, golden brown in that period without burning. Remove the pork with a strainer or slotted spoon to a small baking dish and keep it warm in the oven. Fry the other half and add to the first batch.

To make the sauce, pour off any oil remaining in the wok or use a 10-inch skillet. Set the pan over high heat for about 30 seconds. Pour in the tablespoon of oil, swirl it about in the pan and heat for another 30 seconds, turning the heat down to moderate if the oil begins to smoke. Add the garlic, then the green pepper and carrot, and stir-fry for 2 to 3 minutes until the pepper and carrot darken somewhat in color. Be careful not to let them burn. Pour in the ½ cup of chicken stock, the sugar, vinegar and soy sauce, and bring to a boil. Boil rapidly for about 1 minute, or until the sugar has thoroughly dissolved. Immediately give the cornstarch mixture a quick stir to recombine it and add it to the pan. Cook a moment longer, stirring constantly. When the sauce is thick and clear, pour the entire contents of the pan over the fried pork and serve at once.

As a main course, this will serve 2 to 4. As part of a Chinese meal *(page 120)*, it will serve 4 to 6.

VARIATION: Sweet-and-sour shrimp is made in precisely the same way—with identical batter and sauce. Shell and devein 1 pound of fresh or defrosted frozen shrimp and substitute them for the pork in this recipe.

Hung-shao-ti-pang 紅燒蹄膀
RED-COOKED PORK SHOULDER

6 dried Chinese mushrooms, 1 to 1½ inches in diameter
A 4- to 5-pound fresh pork picnic shoulder or cala with the rind left on
½ cup soy sauce
1 whole star anise or 8 sections of star anise

2 tablespoons light or dark rock candy, broken into ¼-inch pieces, or 2 tablespoons granulated sugar
¼ cup Chinese rice wine, or pale dry sherry
2 cups cold water
2 scallions, including the green tops, cut in 3-inch lengths

PREPARE AHEAD: In a small bowl, cover the mushrooms with ½ cup of warm water and let them soak for 30 minutes. Remove them with a slotted spoon and discard the water. With a cleaver or sharp knife, cut away and discard the tough stems of the mushrooms, and leave the caps whole.

TO COOK: Place the pork shoulder in a heavy pot or saucepan just large enough to hold it snugly. To blanch the pork, add enough cold water to cover it by 2 inches and, over high heat, bring the water to a boil. Let it boil briskly for 5 minutes, then transfer the meat from the pot to a colander and run hot tap water over it. Discard the cooking water and replace the meat in the pot. Add the soy sauce, star anise, rock candy, wine, scallions and 2 cups of cold water. Bring to a boil and cover the pot. Reduce the heat to low and cook the meat for about 3 hours, adjusting the heat to keep the liquid at a simmer and turning the meat over 2 or 3 times during the cooking period. Then add the soaked mushrooms and cook 30 minutes longer. There should be about 1 cup of liquid left when the meat has finished cooking. If there is more, cook uncovered until the liquid is reduced.

Traditionally, the meat is served by transferring it to a deep platter and pouring the cooking juices over it. Decorate the cooked shoulder with the mushrooms. The rind and pork should be soft enough to be pulled off the bone with chopsticks or a fork. Less traditionally, the bone may be removed from the shoulder, and the meat (with the rind on) carved into slices and the sauce poured over it. As a main course, the red-cooked pork will serve 6 to 8. As part of a Chinese meal *(page 120)*, it will serve 8 to 10.

Chen-chu-jou-wan

珍珠肉丸

PEARL BALLS

½ cup glutinous rice
4 dried Chinese mushrooms, 1 to 1½
    inches in diameter
1 pound lean boneless pork, finely
    ground
1 egg, lightly beaten
1 tablespoon soy sauce
1½ teaspoons salt

½ teaspoon sugar
1 teaspoon finely chopped, peeled
    fresh ginger root
6 canned water chestnuts, drained and
    finely chopped
1 scallion, including the green top,
    finely chopped

PREPARE AHEAD: 1. In a small bowl, cover the rice with 1 cup of cold water and soak for 2 hours. Then drain the rice through a sieve, spread it out on a cloth towel and let it dry.

2. In a small bowl, cover the mushrooms with ½ cup of warm water and let them soak for 30 minutes. Discard the water. With a cleaver or knife, cut away and discard the mushroom stems, and chop the caps fine.

3. Combine the pork, egg, soy sauce, salt and sugar in a mixing bowl. With your fingers or a large spoon, mix together until the ingredients are thoroughly blended. Then add the ginger, chopped mushrooms, water chestnuts and scallions, and mix thoroughly again. Scoop up about 2 tablespoons of the mixture and, with your hands, shape it into a ball 1 inch in diameter. Repeat this process with the remaining pork mixture, moistening your hands from time to time with a little cold water. Arrange the balls side by side on a strip of wax paper.

4. Roll one pork ball at a time in the rice, pressing down gently but firmly as you roll so that the rice grains adhere to the meat. Set the rice-coated balls back on wax paper.

TO COOK: Pour enough boiling water into the lower part of a steamer to come within an inch of the cooking rack (or use a steamer substitute as described on page 8). Choose a heatproof plate about ½ inch smaller in diameter than the pot so that the steam can rise and circulate around the pork balls as they steam. Arrange the pork balls on it. Place the plate on the rack, bring the water in the steamer to a boil, and cover the pan tightly. Keeping the water at a continuous boil and replenishing it if it boils away, steam the pork balls for 30 minutes. Set the steaming plate on a large platter and serve at once. As a main course, this recipe will serve 4. As part of a Chinese meal *(page 120)*, it will serve 6 to 8.

Liang-pan-yao-pien

涼拌腰片

SPICED PORK KIDNEY SALAD

6 pork kidneys
1 tablespoon peanut oil, or flavorless
vegetable oil
1 tablespoon finely shredded, peeled
fresh ginger root
1 scallion, including the green top,

finely chopped
1/2 teaspoon cayenne pepper
2 tablespoons soy sauce
2 teaspoons white vinegar
1 teaspoon sugar
2 teaspoons sesame-seed oil

PREPARE AHEAD: 1. With a cleaver or sharp knife, peel off the thin white tissue covering the kidneys if the butcher has not already removed it. Split the kidneys in half lengthwise. Then, with the cut surfaces up, slice off another 1/4 inch from the center of each half to remove the tough membranes and the fat. Lay each kidney flat side down on a chopping board and, holding it firmly with one hand, cut it horizontally into paper-thin slices.

2. In a bowl, cover the kidneys with cold water and let them soak for at least an hour, changing the water twice.

3. To blanch the kidneys, drain them thoroughly, return them to the bowl and pour 1 quart of boiling water over them. Drain, pour a second quart of boiling water over them and drain again.

4. Have the kidneys, oil, ginger, scallions, cayenne pepper, soy sauce, vinegar, sugar and sesame-seed oil within easy reach.

TO COOK: Set a 12-inch wok or 10-inch skillet over high heat for 30 seconds. Pour in the oil, swirl it about in the pan and heat for another 30 seconds, turning the heat down to moderate if the oil begins to smoke. Add the ginger, scallions and cayenne pepper. Stir-fry for 1 minute, then add the kidneys, soy sauce, vinegar and sugar. Stir-fry for about 30 seconds, or only long enough to heat them through. Turn off the heat under the pan and stir in the sesame-seed oil. Transfer the entire contents of the pan to a platter, cool to room temperature and serve. As a first course or side dish, this will serve 6 to 8. As part of a Chinese meal *(page 120)*, it will serve 10 to 12.

K'ao-pai-ku
BARBECUED SPARERIBS

烤排骨

2 pounds spareribs in one piece

MARINADE
¼ cup soy sauce
2 tablespoons honey
2 tablespoons *hoisin* sauce
2 tablespoons white vinegar

1 tablespoon Chinese rice wine, or
   pale dry sherry
1 teaspoon finely chopped garlic
1 teaspoon sugar
2 tablespoons chicken stock, fresh or
   canned
Canned plum sauce

PREPARE AHEAD: 1. With a cleaver or large, sharp knife, trim any excess fat from the spareribs. If the breastbone is still attached, use a cleaver to chop it away from the ribs and discard it. Place the spareribs in a long, shallow dish, large enough to hold them comfortably.

2. In a small bowl, combine the soy sauce, honey, *hoisin* sauce, vinegar, wine, garlic, sugar and chicken stock. Stir until they are well mixed. Pour the sauce over the spareribs, baste them thoroughly and let them marinate for 3 hours at room temperature (6 hours if refrigerated), turning them over in the marinade and basting them every hour or so.

TO COOK: Preheat the oven to 375°. To catch the drippings of the spareribs as they roast, and to prevent the oven from smoking as well, fill a large shallow roasting pan or baking dish with water and place it on the lowest rack of the oven. Insert the curved tips of two or three S-shaped hooks—such as curtain hooks or 5-inch lengths of heavy-duty wire or even unpainted coat hangers bent into shape—at each end of the spareribs. As if hanging a hammock, use the curved ends of the hooks to suspend the ribs from the uppermost rack of the oven directly above the pan of water. Roast the ribs undisturbed for 45 minutes. Then raise the oven heat to 450° and roast about 15 minutes longer, or until the spareribs are crisp and a deep, golden brown.

To serve, place the ribs on a chopping board and, with a cleaver, separate the strip into individual ribs. If the ribs are large, chop them each in half crosswise. Serve hot or cold with plum sauce. As a main course, this will serve 4 to 6. As part of an elaborate Chinese meal *(page 120)*, it will serve 6 to 8.

Yang-ts'ung-pai-ku

洋葱排骨

BRAISED PORK CHOPS WITH ONIONS

To serve 6

6 lean loin pork chops, preferably
   center cut, ½ inch thick
3 tablespoons soy sauce
1 teaspoon sugar
1 tablespoon Chinese rice wine, or

pale dry sherry
2 teaspoons flour
2 tablespoons peanut oil, or
   flavorless vegetable oil
3 medium onions, peeled and finely
   shredded
2 tablespoons cold water

PREPARE AHEAD: 1. With a cleaver or sharp knife, trim most of the fat from the pork chops. On a chopping board, pound each chop with the flat side of the cleaver or a meat mallet, then turn them over and pound them again to make them as thin as possible.

2. In a mixing bowl, combine 2 tablespoons of soy sauce, the sugar and wine, stir together thoroughly, and pour over the pork chops. Coat the chops thoroughly with the sauce, then lay them side by side on a sheet of wax paper.

3. Using a fine strainer or your fingers, sprinkle each chop with a light dusting of flour, then turn the chops over and flour the other side.

4. Have the chops, oil, shredded onions and 2 tablespoons of water within easy reach.

TO COOK: Set a 12-inch wok or 10-inch skillet over high heat for 30 seconds. Pour in the 2 tablespoons of oil, swirl it about in the pan and heat for another 30 seconds, turning the heat down to moderate if the oil begins to smoke. Add 3 pork chops and cook them for 2 minutes on each side until they are golden brown. With tongs or chopsticks, transfer the browned chops to a plate, then brown the remaining chops and transfer these to the plate. Add the shredded onions to the oil remaining in the pan and stir-fry over moderate heat for 1 minute until they are translucent but not brown. Return the chops to the pan, sprinkle the remaining tablespoon of soy sauce and 2 tablespoons of water over them, and cover the pan tightly. Reduce the heat to low, and cook the chops and onions for 20 minutes. Turn the chops over and cook 10 minutes longer. To serve, transfer the chops to a large heated platter and spread the onions over them.

Kan-shao-nu-jou-ssŭ　　　　　乾燒牛肉絲

STIR-FRIED FLANK STEAK WITH CELLOPHANE NOODLES

Half of a 2-ounce package of
 cellophane noodles
½ pound flank steak
2 tablespoons soy sauce
1 teaspoon cornstarch
½ teaspoon sugar
2 cups peanut oil, or flavorless
 vegetable oil

1 green pepper, seeded, deribbed
 and shredded into strips 1½ to 2
 inches long and ¼ inch wide
1 teaspoon finely shredded fresh
 ginger root
¼ to ½ teaspoon cayenne pepper,
 according to taste

PREPARE AHEAD: 1. With a sharp knife or a pair of scissors, cut the cellophane noodles into 4-inch lengths, separating any noodles that cling together.

2. With a cleaver or sharp, heavy knife, trim off and discard the fat from the flank steak. To shred the steak, put it in the freezer for 30 minutes or so to firm the meat and make it easier to slice. Then lay the steak flat on a chopping board and slice the meat horizontally (with the grain) as thin as possible. Cut these slices into pieces 1½ to 2 inches long and ⅛ inch wide.

3. In a small bowl combine the soy sauce, cornstarch and sugar. Add the shredded steak and toss it about in the bowl until it is well coated with the mixture.

4. Have the noodles, steak, oil, green pepper, ginger and cayenne pepper within easy reach.

TO COOK: Set a 12-inch wok or 10-inch skillet over high heat and pour in the 2 cups of oil. Heat the oil until it smokes, or it registers 450° on a deep-frying thermometer. Drop in half of the noodles and let them deep-fry for one second. As soon as they puff up, lift them out with a slotted spoon and spread them on a double thickness of paper towels to drain. Then fry the other half of the noodles. Pour off the oil and set it aside in a small mixing bowl.

Return the wok or skillet to the heat and return 1 tablespoon of the oil to the pan. Swirl it about in the pan and let it heat for 30 seconds, turning the heat down to moderate if the oil begins to smoke. Drop in the green pepper and stir-fry for 2 minutes until it begins to darken in color. With a slotted spoon, transfer the green pepper to a plate. Add another 2 tablespoons of oil to the pan and let it heat for 30 seconds. Add the ginger root, and stir it about for 1 or 2 seconds, then add the shredded flank steak and cayenne pepper, and stir-fry for 1 to 2 minutes, until the beef is lightly browned and any liquid which may have accumulated in the pan has completely evaporated. Return the green pepper to the pan and heat it through, stirring constantly.

74

To serve, place the beef and pepper mixture in the center of a large heated platter and arrange the fried cellophane noodles around the outside. As a main course, this will serve 2. As part of a Chinese meal *(page 120)*, it will serve 4.

Hung-shao-niu-jou

红烧牛肉

BRAISED SOY SAUCE BEEF

2 pounds lean, boneless beef,
   preferably chuck or shin
1 cup water
3 tablespoons soy sauce
2 tablespoons Chinese rice wine, or

   pale dry sherry
1 tablespoon sugar
1 teaspoon salt
3 tablespoons peanut oil, or flavorless
   vegetable oil

PREPARE AHEAD: 1. With a cleaver or sharp knife, trim away and discard all the fat from the beef. Cut the meat into 1½-inch cubes and pat them thoroughly dry with paper towels.

2. Combine the water, soy sauce, wine, sugar and salt in a small bowl.

3. Have the beef, the liquid mixture and oil within easy reach.

TO COOK: Set a 12-inch wok or 10-inch skillet over high heat for about 30 seconds. Pour in 2 tablespoons of oil, swirl it about in the pan and heat again for 30 seconds, turning the heat down to moderate if the oil begins to smoke. Drop in half of the meat cubes and stir-fry over high heat for 2 minutes, or until the pieces are lightly brown on all sides. Then transfer them with a slotted spoon to a heavy 2- to 3-quart saucepan. Add the remaining 1 tablespoon of oil to the pan and brown the rest of the meat. When the cubes are browned, return the first batch to the pan, add the liquid mixture and toss together thoroughly so that the meat is well moistened. Bring to a boil over high heat, cover the pan and reduce the heat to low. Let the meat cook for about 1½ hours, adjusting the heat to keep the liquids simmering slowly and stirring occasionally to prevent the meat from sticking to the pan. The liquid will reduce to about ½ cup of rich sauce. Serve the meat on a heated platter with its sauce poured over it. As a main course, this will serve 4 to 6. As part of a Chinese meal *(page 120)*, it will serve 6 to 8.

Chin-ch'ien-niu-pai

金錢牛排

STIR-FRIED BEEF TENDERLOIN WITH VEGETABLES

4 dried Chinese mushrooms, 1 to 1½
   inches in diameter
¼ cup fresh snow peas (thoroughly
   defrosted frozen snow peas will do
   but they will not have the crispness
   of the fresh ones)
1 pound beef tenderloin
1 teaspoon sugar
2 tablespoons soy sauce
1 tablespoon Chinese rice wine, or

pale dry sherry
2 teaspoons cornstarch
6 peeled fresh water chestnuts or
   rinsed, drained canned ones, sliced
   ¼ inch thick
3 tablespoons peanut oil, or flavorless
   vegetable oil
4 slices peeled fresh ginger root, about
   1 inch in diameter and ⅛ inch thick
½ teaspoon salt

PREPARE AHEAD: 1. In a small bowl, cover the mushrooms with ½ cup of warm water and let them soak for 30 minutes. Remove them with a slotted spoon and discard the water. With a cleaver or sharp knife, cut away and discard the tough stems of the mushrooms, and cut each cap into quarters.

2. Snap off the tips of the fresh snow peas. String the pea pods and blanch them in the following fashion: Drop them into a quart of boiling water. They will turn bright green in 1 minute. Immediately drain and run cold water over them to stop their cooking and set their color. Frozen snow peas need only be thoroughly defrosted.

3. With a cleaver or heavy, sharp knife, trim away and discard any fat from the tenderloin of beef, and cut the meat into 1-inch cubes.

4. In a bowl, combine the sugar, soy sauce, wine and cornstarch, and mix them together thoroughly. Add the beef cubes and toss them about in the bowl with a large spoon until they are coated with the mixture.

5. Have the above ingredients, the oil, ginger and salt within easy reach.

TO COOK: Set a 12-inch wok or 10-inch skillet over high heat for 30 seconds. Pour in 1 tablespoon of oil, swirl it about in the pan and heat for another 30 seconds, turning the heat down to moderate if the oil begins to smoke. Add the mushrooms, snow peas and water chestnuts, and stir-fry over moderate heat for about 2 minutes, or until all the ingredients are coated with the oil. Stir in the salt, then remove the vegetables with a slotted spoon and set them aside on a plate. Pour the remaining 2 tablespoons of oil into the pan, add the ginger and turn the heat to high. Drop in the beef cubes and stir-fry for 2 to 3 minutes, or until they are lightly browned on all sides. Pick out and discard the ginger, and return the reserved vegetables to the pan. Stirring constantly, cook them for about 10 seconds, or only long enough to heat the vegetables through. Transfer the entire contents of the pan to a platter and serve at once. As a main course, this will serve 2 to 4. As part of a Chinese meal (page 120), it will serve 4 to 6.

Hao-shih-niu-jou

蠔豉牛肉

STIR-FRIED GROUND BEEF WITH SMOKED OYSTERS

½ cup shelled fresh peas (or substitute thoroughly defrosted frozen peas)
1 tablespoon soy sauce
1 tablespoon Chinese rice wine, or pale dry sherry
1 teaspoon cornstarch
12 lettuce leaves (Bibb, Boston or iceberg)
2 tablespoons peanut oil, or flavorless

vegetable oil
½ pound lean boneless beef, preferably top round, ground once
1 3¼-ounce can smoked oysters, drained and finely chopped
1 tablespoon bottled oyster sauce
1 teaspoon cornstarch dissolved in 1 tablespoon cold chicken stock, fresh or canned, or cold water

PREPARE AHEAD: 1. Blanch the freshly shelled peas by dropping them into 4 cups of rapidly boiling water and letting them boil uncovered for 5 to 10 minutes, or until tender. Then drain and run cold water over them to stop their cooking and set their color. Frozen peas need only be thoroughly defrosted.

2. Combine in a bowl the soy sauce, wine and 1 teaspoon cornstarch, and stir until the cornstarch is dissolved. Add the ground beef and mix together with your fingers or a spoon until the ingredients are thoroughly combined.

3. Separate the lettuce leaves, wash them under cold running water and pat them dry with paper towels. Cut them into 5-inch rounds. Arrange the leaves on a serving platter and refrigerate.

4. Have the above ingredients, the oil, oysters, oyster sauce and cornstarch mixture within easy reach.

TO COOK: Set a 12-inch wok or 10-inch skillet over high heat for 30 seconds. Pour in the 2 tablespoons of oil, swirl it about in the pan and heat for another 30 seconds, turning the heat down to moderate if the oil begins to smoke. Add the ground beef and stir-fry for about 1 minute, or until it loses its red color and any liquid which has accumulated in the pan evaporates. Add the peas, oysters and oyster sauce. Stir-fry for a minute longer, then give the cornstarch mixture a quick stir to recombine it and add it to the pan. Cook, stirring, for a few seconds until the ingredients are coated with a light, clear glaze. Immediately transfer the entire contents of the pan to a heated platter and serve at once, accompanied by the lettuce leaves.

Traditionally, each guest spreads a lettuce leaf on his plate and places about 2 tablespoons of the beef mixture in the middle of the leaf. The leaf is folded in half over the beef and tucked gently under it, one end of the package is then folded over about 1 inch to enclose the filling securely, and the whole rolled into a neat cylinder that can be picked up with the fingers and eaten. As a main course, this will serve 2 to 4. As part of an elaborate Chinese meal *(page 120)*, it will serve 4 to 6.

Tung-yang-jou

凍羊肉

JELLIED LAMB

This is a modernized version of a classic Chinese dish. The original recipe did not, of course, use packaged gelatin but fresh pork rind, chopped fine and cooked for hours until it turned to jelly.

1 pound lean boneless lamb
4 large garlic cloves, unpeeled
1 teaspoon salt
2 teaspoons soy sauce
¼ cup Chinese rice wine, or pale dry

sherry
1 whole star anise or 8 sections of
   star anise
1 envelope unflavored gelatin
¼ cup cold water

PREPARE AHEAD: 1. With a cleaver or sharp knife, trim the lamb of any fat and cut the meat into 1-inch cubes.

2. Crush the garlic cloves, one at a time, by placing the flat of a cleaver, the side of a large knife blade or even a wooden kitchen mallet over a clove and giving it a sharp blow with your fist. Remove and discard the garlic peel.

3. In a heavy 1- to 2-quart saucepan, combine the lamb, salt, soy sauce, garlic, wine, star anise and enough cold water to cover the lamb pieces. Bring to a boil over high heat, skimming off any foam or scum as it rises to the surface. Then reduce the heat to low and simmer the lamb, partially covered, for about 1½ hours, or until the meat is soft enough to be shredded with chopsticks or a fork. Then remove and discard the garlic cloves and star anise, and, with a slotted spoon, transfer the cubes of lamb to a large mixing bowl, shred the cubes into tiny pieces and set the cooking liquid aside.

4. Pour the unflavored gelatin into ¼ cup of cold water and let it soften for about 5 minutes.

5. Stir the softened gelatin into the lamb's cooking liquid, bring to a boil and simmer, stirring constantly, a moment or two until the gelatin has completely dissolved. Turn off the heat and stir in the pieces of lamb. Pour the mixture into a 2½-by-5-inch loaf mold or 1-quart heatproof bowl. Refrigerate for at least 4 hours, or until it has set and is completely firm.

TO SERVE: Run a sharp knife around the inside of the mold to loosen the jellied lamb around the edges, and dip the bottom of the mold in hot water for a few seconds. Then wipe the outside of the mold completely dry, place a chilled serving plate upside down over the mold and, grasping both sides firmly, turn the plate and mold over. Rap the plate on a table, and the jellied lamb should slide easily out of the mold. If it does not, repeat the entire process. Cut the lamb into ½-inch slices and arrange these in a row down the center of a platter, overlapping them slightly. Serve chilled.

As a main course, this recipe will serve 3 or 4. As part of a Chinese meal (*page 120*), it will serve 6 to 8.

Wu-hsiang-niu-jou 五香牛肉
BRAISED STAR ANISE BEEF

2 pounds boneless beef shin
3 to 4 cups cold water
5 tablespoons soy sauce
2 tablespoons Chinese rice wine, or
    pale dry sherry
2 tablespoons sugar

4 slices peeled fresh ginger root,
    about 1 inch in diameter and ⅛
    inch thick
1 whole star anise or 8 sections of
    star anise
1 tablespoon sesame-seed oil

Place the beef in a heavy 3- to 4-quart saucepan and pour in 3 to 4 cups of cold water—enough to just cover the meat. Bring to a boil over high heat and, as the scum begins to rise to the surface of the water, skim it carefully. Then stir in the soy sauce, wine, sugar, ginger and star anise, and partially cover the pan. Reduce the heat to moderate and cook the beef, adjusting the heat to keep the liquid at a simmer, for 2½ to 3 hours, or until it shows no resistance when pierced with the tip of a sharp knife. There should be about 1 cup of cooking liquid left in the pan. If there is more, remove the cover and increase the heat somewhat, and cook until the liquid is reduced. Add the sesame-seed oil and simmer slowly for another 10 minutes.

When the meat is done, transfer it to a carving board and, with a cleaver or sharp knife, cut it into the thinnest possible slices. Arrange them attractively in overlapping layers on a heated platter. Remove and discard the ginger and star anise, and pour the braising sauce over the beef.

Or you may, if you wish, serve the beef cold. In that event, let the unsliced beef cool in the sauce. Then refrigerate it until you are ready to serve it. Carve the beef into paper-thin slices and serve it with or without the braising sauce.

As a main course, this recipe will serve 4 to 6. As part of a Chinese meal (*page 120*), it will serve 8 to 10.

Ching-chiao-ch'ao-niu-jou

青椒炒牛肉

PEPPER STEAK

1 pound flank steak, trimmed of all
    fat
1 tablespoon Chinese rice wine, or
    pale dry sherry
3 tablespoons soy sauce
1 teaspoon sugar
2 teaspoons cornstarch

2 medium-sized green peppers,
    seeded, deribbed and cut into 1/2-
    inch squares
4 slices peeled fresh ginger root, about
    1 inch in diameter and 1/8 inch thick
1/4 cup peanut oil, or flavorless
    vegetable oil

PREPARE AHEAD: 1. With a cleaver or sharp knife, cut the flank steak lengthwise into strips 1½ inches wide, then crosswise into ¼-inch slices.

2. In a large bowl, mix the wine, soy sauce, sugar and cornstarch. Add the steak slices and toss with a large spoon to coat them thoroughly. The steak may be cooked at once, or marinated for as long as 6 hours.

3. Place the peppers, ginger root and oil within easy reach.

TO COOK: Set a 12-inch wok or 10-inch skillet over high heat for about 30 seconds. Pour in a tablespoon of the oil, swirl it about in the pan and heat for another 30 seconds, turning the heat down to moderate if the oil begins to smoke. Immediately add the pepper squares and stir-fry for 3 minutes, or until they are tender but still crisp. Scoop them out with a slotted spoon and reserve. Pour 3 more tablespoons of oil into the pan and heat almost to the smoking point. Add the ginger, stir for a few seconds, then drop in the steak mixture. Stir-fry over high heat for about 2 minutes, or until the meat shows no sign of pink. Discard the ginger. Add the pepper and cook for a minute, stirring, then transfer the contents of the pan to a heated platter and serve. As a main course, this will serve 2 to 4. As part of a Chinese meal *(page 120)*, it will serve 4 to 6.

Poultry and Eggs

Chiang-yu-chi
BRAISED SOY SAUCE CHICKEN

醬 油 雞

A 4½- to 5-pound roasting chicken, preferably freshly killed
2 cups cold water
2 cups soy sauce
¼ cup Chinese rice wine, or pale dry sherry
5 slices peeled, fresh ginger root
about 1 inch in diameter and ⅛ inch thick
1 whole star anise, or 8 sections star anise
¼ cup rock candy broken into small pieces, or substitute 2 tablespoons granulated sugar
1 teaspoon sesame-seed oil

PREPARE AHEAD: 1. Wash the chicken inside and out under cold running water. Dry the chicken thoroughly with paper towels.

2. Have the water, soy sauce, wine, ginger, anise, rock candy (or sugar) and sesame-seed oil within easy reach.

TO COOK: In a heavy pot just large enough to hold the chicken snugly, bring the water, soy sauce, wine, ginger and star anise to a boil, then add the chicken. The liquid should reach halfway up the side of the chicken. Bring to a boil again, reduce the heat to moderate and cook covered for 20 minutes. With 2 large spoons, turn the chicken over. Stir the rock candy or sugar into the sauce and baste the chicken thoroughly. Simmer 20 minutes longer, basting frequently. Turn off the heat, cover the pot and let the chicken cool for 2 to 3 hours.

Transfer the chicken to a chopping board and brush it with sesame-seed oil. Remove the wings and legs with a cleaver or sharp knife and split the chicken in half lengthwise by cutting through its breastbone and backbone. Lay the halves skin side up on the board and chop them crosswise, bones and all, into 1-by-3-inch pieces, reconstructing the pieces in approximately their original shape in the center of a platter as you proceed. Chop the wings and legs similarly, and place them, reconstructed, around the breasts. Moisten the chicken with ¼ cup of the sauce in which it cooked and serve at room temperature. As a main course, this will serve 4 to 6. As part of a Chinese meal *(page 120)*, it will serve 8 to 10.

NOTE: The sauce in which the chicken cooks is known in China as a master sauce and it is stored in a covered jar for use in red-cooked dishes. It will keep for 2 weeks in the refrigerator, indefinitely in the freezer.

Mo-ku-chi-pien

蔴菇雞片

STIR-FRIED CHICKEN WITH FRESH MUSHROOMS

2 whole chicken breasts, about ¾
  pound each
2 teaspoons cornstarch
1 egg white
1 tablespoon Chinese rice wine, or
  pale dry sherry
1 teaspoon salt
¼ pound fresh snow peas (frozen,
  thoroughly defrosted snow peas
  will do, but they will not have the
  crispness of the fresh ones)

4 tablespoons peanut oil, or flavorless
  vegetable oil
¼ pound fresh mushrooms, about 1
  inch in diameter, sliced ¼ inch
  thick
2 slices peeled fresh ginger root,
  about 1 inch in diameter and ⅛
  inch thick
1 teaspoon cornstarch dissolved in 1
  tablespoon cold chicken stock or
  water

PREPARE AHEAD: 1. One at a time, skin, bone and slice the chicken breasts in the following fashion: Lay the whole unsplit chicken breast on its side on a chopping board. Holding the breast firmly in place with your hand, cut it lengthwise through the skin along the curved breastbone with a cleaver or sharp knife. Carefully free the meat from the bones with the cleaver. Then grasp the meat in one hand, and pull it off the bones and away from the skin—using the cleaver to free the meat if necessary. Turn the breast over and repeat on the other side. Remove each tube-shaped fillet from the boned breast meat, and pull out and discard the tendon in each fillet. Lay the breast meat and fillets flat, and cut them into paper-thin slices. Then cut the slices into pieces about 2 inches long and 1 inch wide.

2. In a large mixing bowl, combine the chicken and cornstarch, and toss them about with a spoon until each piece is lightly coated. Add the egg white, wine and salt, and stir them with the chicken until they are thoroughly mixed together.

3. Snap off the tips of the fresh snow peas and, with a small, sharp knife, string the pea pods.

4. Have the chicken, snow peas, oil, ginger, mushrooms and the cornstarch mixture within easy reach.

TO COOK: Set a 12-inch wok or 10-inch skillet over high heat for about 30 seconds. Pour in 1 tablespoon of oil, swirl it about in the pan and heat for another 30 seconds, turning the heat down to moderate if the oil begins to smoke. Add the mushrooms, snow peas and ½ teaspoon of salt, and stir-fry over moderate heat for about 2 minutes. With a long spoon, transfer the vegetables to a platter and set aside. Add 3 tablespoons of oil to the pan and let it heat for 30 seconds. Drop in the ginger slices, cook for about 30 seconds, then remove and discard them. Immediately, add the chicken and stir-fry for about 2 minutes, or until the pieces are firm and white. Return the reserved cooked vegetables to the pan. Give the cornstarch mixture a quick stir to recombine it, add it to the pan and cook, stirring constantly for a few seconds, until the ingredients are coated with a light, clear glaze. Transfer the entire contents of the pan to a heated platter and serve at once. As a main course, this will serve 4. As part of a Chinese meal *(page 120)*, it will serve 6 to 8.

Cha-pa-kwai
EIGHT-PIECES CHICKEN

炸八塊

A 2½-pound frying chicken
2 tablespoons soy sauce
1 tablespoon Chinese rice wine, or
    pale dry sherry
1 teaspoon salt
½ teaspoon sugar
1 scallion, including the green top,
    cut into 2-inch pieces and split in
    half

A ½-inch cube peeled fresh ginger
    root, crushed with a cleaver or
    kitchen mallet
3 cups peanut oil, or flavorless
    vegetable oil
½ cup flour
Roasted salt and pepper, prepared
    according to the recipe on page
    93

PREPARE AHEAD: 1. On a chopping board, cut off the wings, legs and thighs of the chicken with a cleaver or large, sharp knife. Cut the body in half by cutting down through the breastbone and backbone. Then, one at a time, chop the 8 pieces of chicken across the bones into 2-inch pieces. Spread the chicken on a double thickness of paper towels and pat each piece thoroughly dry.

2. In a large bowl, combine the soy sauce, wine, salt, sugar, scallions and ginger, stirring until the salt and sugar dissolve. Add the chicken and toss the pieces about to coat them thoroughly with the mixture. Marinate at room temperature for 1 to 2 hours.

3. Have the chicken, flour and oil within easy reach.

TO COOK: Pour 3 cups of oil into a 12-inch wok or deep-fryer and heat the oil until a haze forms above it or it registers 375° on a deep-frying thermometer. Drain the chicken and discard the marinade. With paper towels, wipe the chicken pieces dry. Dip them in the flour, then vigorously shake off all but a light dusting of the flour. Drop the chicken into the hot oil and fry, turning the pieces frequently for 5 minutes, or until the pieces are golden brown on both sides. Remove them from the oil with a bamboo strainer or slotted spoon and drain them on a double thickness of paper towels. Serve on a heated platter accompanied by roasted salt and pepper *(page 93)*. As a main course this will serve 2 to 4. As part of a Chinese meal *(page 120)*, it will serve 4 to 6.

Chiang-pao-chi-ting

醬爆雞丁

STIR-FRIED CHICKEN BREASTS WITH HOISIN SAUCE

2 whole chicken breasts, about ¾ pound each

1 tablespoon cornstarch

1 tablespoon Chinese rice wine, or pale dry sherry

1 tablespoon soy sauce

¼ cup peanut oil, or flavorless vegetable oil

1 medium green pepper, deribbed, seeded and cut in ½-inch squares

6 water chestnuts, cut in ¼-inch cubes

¼ pound fresh mushrooms, cut in ¼-inch cubes

½ teaspoon salt

2 tablespoons *hoisin* sauce

¼ cup roasted cashews or almonds

PREPARE AHEAD: 1. One at a time, bone, skin and slice the chicken breasts in the following fashion: Lay the whole chicken breast on its side on a chopping board. Holding the breast firmly in place with your hand, cut it with a cleaver or sharp knife lengthwise through the skin, along the curved breastbone. Carefully cut all the meat from the bones on one side of the breastbone. Then grasp the meat in one hand and pull it off the bones and away from the skin—using the cleaver to free the meat if necessary. Turn the breast over and repeat on the other side. Remove each tube-shaped fillet from the boned breast meat, and pull out and discard the tendon in each fillet. Lay the breast meat and fillets flat and cut them lengthwise into ½-inch strips, then cut the strips crosswise to make ½-inch squares.

2. Place the chicken squares in a large bowl and sprinkle them with cornstarch, then toss them about with a spoon to coat them lightly and evenly. Pour in the wine and soy sauce, and toss the chicken again to coat the squares.

3. Place the above ingredients, and the oil, green pepper, water chestnuts, mushrooms, salt, *hoisin* sauce and cashews or almonds within easy reach.

TO COOK: Set a 12-inch wok or 10-inch skillet over high heat for about 30 seconds. Pour in a tablespoon of the oil, swirl it about in the pan and heat for another 30 seconds, turning the heat down to moderate if the oil begins to smoke. Immediately add the green peppers, water chestnuts, mushrooms and salt, and stir-fry briskly for 2 to 3 minutes. Scoop out the vegetables with a slotted spoon and set them aside on a plate. Pour the remaining 3 tablespoons of oil into the pan, heat almost to the smoking point and drop in the marinated chicken. Stir-fry over high heat for 2 to 3 minutes until the chicken turns white and firm. Then add the *hoisin* sauce, stir well with the chicken, add the reserved vegetables and cook for 1 minute longer. Now drop in the cashews or almonds and stir to heat them through. Transfer the entire contents of the pan to a heated platter and serve at once. As a main course, this will serve 4. As part of a Chinese meal *(page 120)*, it will serve 6 to 8.

Yin-ya-chi-ssu　　　　　　　銀芽雞絲

STIR-FRIED CHICKEN WITH FRESH BEAN SPROUTS

2 whole chicken breasts, about ¾
   pounds each
2 teaspoons cornstarch
1 egg white, lightly beaten
2 teaspoons salt
2 teaspoons Chinese rice wine, or pale
   dry sherry

2 cups fresh bean sprouts (canned
   variety will not do, but you may
   substitute 2 cups finely shredded
   celery)
¼ cup peanut oil, or flavorless
   vegetable oil

PREPARE AHEAD: 1. One at a time, bone, skin and slice the chicken breasts in the following fashion: Lay the whole chicken breast on its side on a chopping board. Holding the breast firmly in place with your hand, cut it with a cleaver or sharp knife lengthwise through the skin, along the curved breastbone. Carefully cut all the meat from the bones on one side of the breastbone. Then grasp the meat in one hand and pull it off the bones and away from the skin—using the cleaver to free the meat if necessary. Turn the breast over and repeat on the other side. Remove each tube-shaped fillet from the boned breast meat, and pull out and discard the white tendon in each fillet. Lay the breast meat and fillets flat and cut them horizontally into paper-thin slices. Then cut the slices into shreds 1½ to 2 inches long and ⅛ inch wide.

2. Place the chicken shreds in a large bowl, sprinkle them with cornstarch and toss to coat lightly. Then add the lightly beaten egg white, 1½ teaspoons of the salt and the wine with a large spoon, mix all the ingredients together gently but thoroughly.

3. Rinse the fresh bean sprouts in a pot of cold water and discard any husks that float to the surface. Drain the sprouts and pat them dry with paper towels.

4. Have the chicken mixture, bean sprouts and oil within easy reach.

TO COOK: Set a 12-inch wok or 10-inch skillet over high heat for about 30 seconds. Pour in 1 tablespoon of oil, swirl it about in the pan and heat for another 30 seconds, turning the heat down to moderate if the oil begins to smoke. Immediately add the bean sprouts and remaining ½ teaspoon salt, and stir-fry for about a minute. Remove them with a bamboo strainer or slotted spoon to a bowl and set aside. Pour the remaining 3 tablespoons of oil into the pan, heat for a few seconds and add the chicken mixture. Stir-fry over high heat for about 1 minute, or until the chicken turns white. Return the bean sprouts to the pan and stir-fry together with the chicken for another minute. Transfer the entire contents of the pan to a heated platter and serve at once. As a main course, this will serve 4 to 6. As part of a Chinese meal (page 120), it will serve 6 to 8.

Yu-lang-chi 玉 蘭 雞

WHITE-CUT CHICKEN AND HAM IN GREEN PARADISE

A 4-pound roasting chicken, preferably freshly killed
3 slices cooked Smithfield ham, ⅛ inch thick, cut into 2-by-1-inch pieces
A 2-pound bunch broccoli
2 quarts chicken stock, fresh or canned, or 2 quarts cold water, or a combination of both

1 scallion, including the green top, cut into 2-inch pieces
4 slices peeled fresh ginger root, about 1 inch in diameter and ⅛ inch thick
¼ teaspoon salt
1 teaspoon cornstarch dissolved in 1 tablespoon cold water

PREPARE AHEAD: 1. Wash the chicken inside and out under cold running water. Dry the chicken thoroughly with paper towels.

2. Cut off the broccoli flowerettes. Peel the stalks by cutting ⅛ inch deep into the skin and stripping it as if you were peeling an onion. Slice the stalks diagonally into 1-inch pieces, discarding the woody ends.

3. Have the chicken, ham, broccoli, chicken stock (or water), scallion, ginger and cornstarch mixture within easy reach.

TO COOK: In a heavy flameproof casserole or pot just large enough to hold the chicken snugly, bring the stock or water to a boil. Add the scallions and ginger, and place the chicken in the pot. The liquid should cover the chicken; add more boiling stock or water if it doesn't. Bring to a boil again, cover the pan, reduce the heat to low and simmer for 15 minutes. Then turn off the heat and let the chicken cool in the covered pot for 2 hours. The residual heat in the pot will cook the chicken through.

Transfer the chicken to a chopping board. (Reserve stock.) With a cleaver or knife, cut off wings and legs, and split the chicken in half lengthwise cutting through the breast and back bones. Cut the meat from the bones, leaving the skin in place. Then cut the meat into pieces about 2 inches long, 1 inch wide and ½ inch thick. Arrange the chicken and ham in alternating overlapped layers on a heated platter and cover with foil.

Pour 2 cups of the reserved stock into a 3-quart saucepan. Bring to a boil and drop in the broccoli. Return to a boil, turn off the heat, let it rest uncovered for 3 minutes, then remove the broccoli and arrange it around the chicken and ham. Or garnish the meat with only the flowerettes and serve the stems separately.

In a small saucepan, combine ½ cup of the stock with salt and bring to a boil. Give the cornstarch mixture a stir to recombine it and add it to the stock. When the stock thickens slightly and becomes clear, pour it over the chicken and ham. Serve at once. As a main course, this will serve 4 to 6. As part of a Chinese meal *(page 120)*, it will serve 8 to 10.

Hsün-chi

燻雞

SMOKED CHICKEN

A 4-pound roasting chicken
2 tablespoons salt

5 tablespoons light or dark brown sugar
1 tablespoon sesame-seed oil

PREPARE AHEAD: Wash the chicken well inside and out under cold running water and pat it dry with paper towels. To flavor and partially cure the chicken, rub it inside and out with the salt, place it in a large bowl or baking dish and refrigerate loosely covered with wax paper for at least 8 hours or overnight.

TO COOK: Pour enough boiling water into the lower part of a steamer to come within an inch of the cooking rack (or use a steamer substitute as described on page 8). Place the chicken on a deep heatproof platter ½ inch smaller in diameter than the pot so that the steam can circulate freely around the chicken as it steams. Bring the water in the steamer to a rolling boil, place the chicken on the rack and cover the pot securely. Keeping the water at a continuous boil and replenishing it as it boils away, steam the chicken for 45 minutes.

With heavy-duty aluminum foil, line the bottom of a deep, heavy casserole just large enough to hold the chicken comfortably. Sprinkle the brown sugar evenly over the foil and place the steamed chicken on a wire rack set over the sugared foil. Line the inside of the casserole lid with more foil, bringing it up over the edges of the lid to ensure its fitting the casserole tightly and to prevent any smoke from escaping. Cover the pot and set it over moderate heat for 10 minutes. Turn off the heat and let the chicken rest for 5 minutes before removing the lid. Lift out the smoked chicken and place it on a chopping board. With a pastry brush, lightly coat the skin with sesame-seed oil, then carve the chicken in the following fashion: Cut off the wings and legs. Divide the body of the chicken in half lengthwise by cutting through the breast and backbone. Lay the halves flat on a board skin side up and, with a cleaver, chop through them, bones and all, at 1-inch intervals. Reconstruct the pieces in their original form in the center of a large platter as you proceed. Then chop the wings and legs into 1-by-3-inch pieces and arrange them similarly reconstructed around the breast. Serve the chicken hot or at room temperature. As a main course, smoked chicken will serve 6 to 8. As part of a Chinese meal (page 120), it will serve 8 to 12.

Ch'ao-chi-kan

STIR-FRIED CHICKEN LIVERS WITH SNOW PEAS 炒雞肝

¼ pound fresh snow peas
  (thoroughly defrosted frozen snow
  peas will do, but they will not have
  the crispness of fresh ones)
½ pound chicken livers
2 tablespoons soy sauce
½ teaspoon sugar
1 tablespoon Chinese rice wine, or
  pale dry sherry

1 teaspoon cornstarch
3 tablespoons peanut oil, or flavorless
  vegetable oil
3 slices peeled fresh ginger root,
  about 1 inch in diameter and ⅛
  inch thick
1 scallion, including the green top,
  cut into 2-inch lengths
½ teaspoon salt

PREPARE AHEAD: 1. Snap the tips off the fresh snow peas, string the pea pods and blanch them in the following fashion: Drop them into a quart of boiling water for 1 minute (they will turn bright green). Immediately drain, and run cold water over them to stop their cooking and set their color. Frozen snow peas need only be thoroughly defrosted.

2. Cut away any clinging membranes from the chicken livers. Wash them quickly under cold water and pat them dry with paper towels. With a cleaver or sharp knife, cut the livers into ½-inch slices.

3. In a bowl, combine the soy sauce, sugar, wine and cornstarch, and mix until the cornstarch is dissolved. Add the livers and, with a spoon, toss them in the mixture until all the pieces are well coated.

4. Have the above ingredients, and the oil, salt, ginger and scallion within easy reach.

TO COOK: Set a 12-inch wok or 10-inch skillet over high heat for about 30 seconds. Pour in the 1 tablespoon of oil, swirl it about in the pan and heat for another 30 seconds, turning the heat down to moderate if the oil begins to smoke. Add the snow peas. Stir-fry for 2 minutes; the peas will remain crisp and will still be bright green. Stir well and remove the peas to a plate. Pour 2 more tablespoons of oil into the pan, raise the heat to high, and add the ginger and the scallion. Stir-fry for 1 minute, drop in the chicken livers and reduce the heat to moderate. Stir-fry the livers for 2 to 3 minutes, or until they are firm and lightly browned. Return the snow peas to the pan, add the salt and cook only long enough to heat them through. Immediately transfer the entire contents of the pan to a heated platter and serve. As a main course, this will serve 2. As part of a Chinese meal (page 120), it will serve 4.

Tsui-chi

醉 雞

DRUNK CHICKEN

A 4-pound chicken, preferably freshly
  killed
6 cups chicken stock, fresh or canned,
  or 6 cups cold water
4 slices peeled fresh ginger root,
  about 1 inch in diameter and

⅛ inch thick
1 scallion, including the green top,
  cut into 2-inch lengths
2 tablespoons salt
1 cup Chinese rice wine, or pale dry
  sherry

PREPARE AHEAD: 1. Place the chicken, breast side up, in a 4- to 5-quart heavy pot or casserole. Pour in the chicken stock or water. The liquid should just cover the chicken; if it doesn't, add more stock or water. Add the ginger and scallion, and bring the liquid to a boil. Then cover the pot, reduce the heat to low and simmer the chicken for 15 minutes. Turn off the heat, leave the cover on the pot and let the chicken cool in its broth for 3 hours. At the end of that period the chicken should be tender. Pour 1 cup of the stock into a small bowl and set it aside to cool. Save the remaining stock for other uses.

2. Transfer the chicken to a chopping block. With a cleaver or large, sharp knife, cut off the wings, legs and thighs of the chicken. Then cut away and discard the backbone, and chop the breast into two pieces along the breastbone. To flavor and partially cure the chicken, sprinkle the 8 pieces on all sides with 2 tablespoons of salt. Arrange the pieces in a shallow glass bowl or enamel baking dish large enough to hold them snugly in one layer.

3. In a bowl, combine the wine and 1 cup of the cooled chicken stock. Pour it over the chicken, cover the dish with plastic wrap or foil and refrigerate for at least a day, preferably for 2 or 3 days. Turn the pieces over occasionally.

TO ASSEMBLE: When ready to serve, drain the chicken of all its liquid. With a cleaver or large, sharp knife, chop the chicken, bones and all, into chunks about 2 inches wide and 1 inch long. Arrange on a platter and serve cold. As a main course, this will serve 4. As an hors d'oeuvre or part of a Chinese cold plate, it will serve 8 to 10.

Sung-tzu-chi-ssu

松子雞絲

STIR-FRIED CHICKEN WITH PINE NUTS AND HOT PEPPERS

2 whole chicken breasts about ¾
  pound each
½ cup pine nuts (pignolia nuts)
2 teaspoons cornstarch
1 egg white
1½ teaspoons salt
1 tablespoon Chinese rice wine, or
  pale dry sherry
½ teaspoon sugar
8-12 lettuce leaves (Boston, Bibb or
  iceberg)
4 tablespoons peanut oil, or flavorless
  vegetable oil
3 small, fresh, hot chili peppers, finely
  shredded
1 teaspoon finely shredded, peeled
  fresh ginger root
1 teaspoon cornstarch dissolved in 1
  tablespoon cold chicken stock, fresh
  or canned, or cold water

PREPARE AHEAD: 1. One at a time, bone, skin and shred the chicken breasts in the following fashion: Lay the whole chicken breast on its side on a chopping board. Holding the breast firmly in place with your hand, cut it lengthwise through the skin along the curved breastbone with a cleaver or sharp knife. Carefully free the meat from the bones with the cleaver. Then grasp the meat in one hand, and pull it off the bones and away from the skin—using the cleaver to free the meat if necessary. Turn the breast over and repeat on the other side. Remove each tube-shaped fillet from the boned breast meat, and pull out and discard the white tendon in each fillet. Lay the breast meat and fillets flat, and cut them horizontally into paper-thin slices. Now cut the slices into shreds about ⅛ inch wide and 1½ to 2 inches long.

2. Preheat the oven to 350°. Spread the pine nuts evenly on a jelly-roll pan or baking sheet and bake them in the center of the oven for about 5 minutes, or until they are lightly speckled with brown. Be careful not to let them burn. Reserve them in a bowl.

3. Place the 2 teaspoons of cornstarch in a small bowl, add the chicken shreds and toss them about until they are lightly coated. Add the egg white, salt, wine and sugar, and stir them with the chicken until they are thoroughly mixed together.

4. Separate the lettuce leaves, wash them under cold running water and pat them dry with paper towels. Arrange them on a serving platter and refrigerate.

5. Have the above ingredients, and the chili peppers, ginger and cornstarch mixture within easy reach.

TO COOK: Set a 12-inch wok or 10-inch skillet over high heat for 30 seconds. Pour in 1 tablespoon of the oil, swirl it about in the pan and heat for another 30 seconds, turning the heat down to moderate if the oil begins to smoke. Add the chili peppers, stir-fry for a minute, then scoop them out with a slotted spoon and set them aside in a small dish. Pour the remaining 3 tablespoons of the oil into the pan, heat for 30 seconds and add the ginger. Stir for a few seconds and drop in the chicken mixture. Stir-fry over moderate heat for 1 or 2 minutes, or until the chicken turns firm and white. Stir in the chili peppers and cook only long enough —about 10 seconds—to heat the peppers through. Give the cornstarch mixture a quick stir to recombine it and pour it in the pan. Cook for a few seconds, stirring constantly, until all the ingredients are coated with a light, clear glaze. Immediately transfer the entire contents of the pan to a heated platter, and serve at once with the pine nuts sprinkled on top as a garnish and the lettuce leaves arranged attractively on another plate as wrappers for the chicken mixture.

To eat, each guest picks up a lettuce leaf in one hand or lays it flat on a plate. About 2 tablespoonfuls of the chicken mixture are then placed in the center of the leaf and the leaf is folded in half, enclosing the chicken within it. The lettuce is rolled into a loose cylinder that can be held in the fingers and eaten. As a main course, this will serve 4 to 6. As part of a Chinese meal *(page 120)*, it will serve 6 to 8 or even 10.

Cha-yeh-tan 茶葉蛋
TEA LEAF EGGS

6 eggs	star anise
1 tablespoon salt	2 teaspoons black tea (or substitute
2 tablespoons soy sauce	2 tea bags)
1 whole star anise or 8 sections	

TO COOK: In a 1½- to 2-quart saucepan, cover the eggs with 2 cups of cold water, bring to a simmer and cook uncovered for 20 minutes. Leave the eggs in the water until they are cool enough to handle, then pour off the water and tap the eggs gently all over with the back of the spoon until the shells are covered with a network of fine cracks. Now return the eggs to the saucepan, pour in 2 cups of cold water, add the salt, soy sauce, star anise and tea. Bring to a boil over high heat, then reduce the heat to its lowest point, cover the pan and simmer for 2 to 3 hours. Check from time to time and if the liquid is cooking away, add enough boiling water to keep the eggs constantly covered. Turn off the heat and leave the eggs in the liquid at room temperature for at least 8 hours.

TO SERVE: Just before serving the eggs, remove their shells carefully. The whites should be marbled with fine, dark lines. Cut the eggs in halves or quarters and arrange them on a plate. Tea leaf eggs are usually served as an hors d'oeuvre, or they may be part of a Chinese cold plate combined with various meats and salads.

Hsiang-su-ya

SZECHWAN DUCK

香酥鴨

A 4- to 5-pound duck
2 tablespoons salt
1 tablespoon whole Szechwan
   peppercorns, crushed with a cleaver
   or with a pestle in a mortar
4 slices peeled fresh ginger root,
   about 1 inch in diameter and ¼
   inch thick
2 scallions, including the green tops,
   cut into 2-inch pieces
2 tablespoons soy sauce
1 teaspoon five-spice powder
3 cups peanut oil, or flavorless
   vegetable oil
Roasted salt and pepper, prepared
   according to recipe opposite
Steamed flower rolls, prepared
   according to recipe on page 9

PREPARE AHEAD: 1. Wash the duck thoroughly under cold running water, then pat it completely dry, inside and out, with paper towels. Place the duck on a table or chopping board, breast side up, and with the palms of both your hands press down hard on the breastbone to break it and flatten it.

2. In a small bowl, combine the salt, crushed peppercorns, scallions and ginger. With a large spoon or your hands, rub the seasonings together to release their flavors. Rub the duck inside and out with the mixture, finally pressing the ginger and scallions firmly against the skin and inside the cavity of the duck to make them adhere. Place the duck on a platter and refrigerate it covered with aluminum foil or plastic wrap for at least 6 hours or overnight.

3. Before cooking, mix the soy sauce and five-spice powder thoroughly together in a small bowl, and rub it over the skin and inside the cavity of the duck.

4. Pour enough boiling water into the lower part of a steamer to come to within an inch of the cooking rack (or use a steamer substitute as described on page 8). Place the duck on its back on a deep, heatproof platter ½ inch smaller in diameter than the pot so that the steam can freely circulate around the duck. Place the platter on the rack, cover the pot securely and bring the water in the steamer to a rolling boil. Keeping the water at a continuous boil, steam the duck for 2 hours. Keep a kettle of water at a boil all the time the duck is steaming, and use this to replenish the water in the steamer as it boils away. Turn off the heat. Let the duck rest in the tightly covered steamer for 30 minutes, then turn the bird over on its breast. Re-cover the steamer and let the duck rest for 30 minutes longer. Transfer the duck from the steamer to a platter lined with a double thickness of paper towels. Brush off and discard the scallion pieces and ginger slices, and place the duck in a cool, airy place to dry for 3 hours or longer.

TO COOK: Pour 3 cups of oil into a 12-inch wok or heavy deep-fryer

and heat it until a haze forms above it or it reaches a temperature of 375°
on a deep-frying thermometer. With two large spoons, carefully lower the
duck into the hot oil on its back and fry it for about 15 minutes. Keep
the 375° temperature as constant as you can and move the duck about
from time to time with chopsticks or two slotted spoons to prevent it
from sticking to either the bottom or sides of the pan. Then turn the
duck over on its breast and deep-fry it, moving it in the same fashion,
for another 15 minutes.

When the duck is a deep golden brown on all sides, carefully transfer
it to a chopping board. With a cleaver or large, sharp knife, cut off the
wings, legs and thighs of the duck and chop them across the bone in 2-
inch pieces. Then cut away and discard the backbone and chop the
breast, bone and all, into 2-inch squares. Arrange the duck pieces attractively on a large heated platter and serve at once with roasted salt and
pepper and steamed flower-roll buns.

As a main course this will serve 6. As part of a Chinese meal *(page 120)*,
it will serve 8 to 10.

Hua-chiao-yen　　　　　　　　　　　　　花椒塩
ROASTED SALT AND PEPPER

To make about ¼ cup

5 tablespoons salt
1 tablespoon whole Szechwan

peppercorns
½ teaspoon whole black
   peppercorns

Set a heavy 5- or 6-inch skillet over high heat, and pour in the salt and
all the peppercorns. Turn the heat down to moderate and cook, stirring constantly, for 5 minutes, or until the mixture browns lightly. Be careful not
to let it burn. Crush it to a fine powder with a mortar and pestle or wrap
the mixture in wax paper and crush it with a kitchen mallet. Shake the
crushed salt and pepper mixture through a fine sieve or strainer into a
small bowl and serve it as a dip for Szechwan duck *(opposite)* or deep-fried
phoenix-tailed shrimp *(page 58)*.

Eight Steps to Bone an Eight-Jewel Duck

Allow 30 minutes to bone a duck, although chances are you'll finish in less time. If frozen, be sure the duck is thoroughly defrosted. Remove neck, giblets and any loose fat; wipe the duck completely dry inside and out with paper towels. For boning, use any kitchen scissors or knife with which you are familiar so long as it is relatively heavy, has a sharp point and finely honed cutting edge.

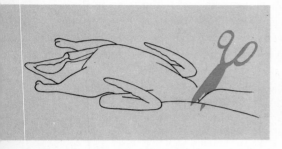

1 Pull the neck skin taut and cut it off to within an inch or so of the body, using kitchen scissors as shown or a sharp, heavy knife.

2 Fold remaining neck skin as far back as it will go and, with tiny snips or cuts, free meat around the neck cavity from the carcass.

3 Wiggle each wing to find the joint where it meets the carcass, then cut through the joint to detach the wing. Leave the wing itself intact.

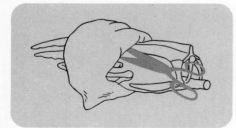

4 Continue to free the meat from the carcass with tiny snips or cuts, turning the duck over and rolling the skin back as you work.

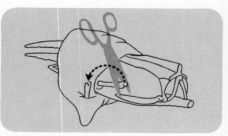

5 Free the meat around each thigh and cut the joint to detach the drumstick from the thigh. Leave the thigh bones on the carcass.

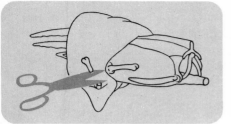 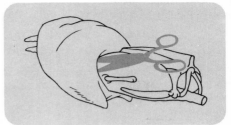

6 Free the meat halfway down the length of the drumstick bone, then cut off and remove the exposed half of the bone. Leave the bottom intact.

7 Cut the meat away from the rest of the carcass, always cutting as close to the bones as you can. Try never to pierce the duck's skin.

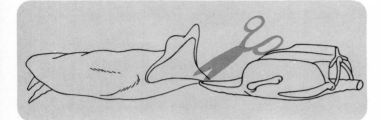

8 Cut through the joint where the tail bone is attached to the backbone of the duck, leaving the tail with the skin and meat. Then turn the skin of the now boned duck right side out again. The Chinese keep the wing bones and the tips of the drumsticks intact to make the finished eight-jewel duck—after it has been stuffed and roasted—look like a whole bird. In thrifty Chinese style, you can use the carcass, other bones and giblets for duck stock (following the chicken stock recipe on page 20), and render the fat.

Pa-pao-ya
EIGHT-JEWEL DUCK

八寶鴨

To serve 8

1 cup glutinous rice
2 dried Chinese mushrooms, 1 to 1½ inches in diameter
10 or 12 dried shrimp
A 4- to 5-pound duck
1 cup quartered, canned whole water-pack French or Italian chestnuts
2 tablespoons peanut oil, or flavorless vegetable oil
¼ pound lean, boneless pork, finely ground
½ teaspoon sugar

1 tablespoon Chinese rice wine, or pale dry sherry
2 tablespoons soy sauce
¼ cup canned whole gingko nuts
3 peeled and washed fresh water chestnuts or drained canned water chestnuts, sliced ⅛ inch thick
A ¼-inch-thick slice of cooked Smithfield ham, cut into ¼-inch dice
2 teaspoons salt
Fresh Chinese parsley sprigs (cilantro), or substitute fresh curly or flat-leaf parsley

Continued on next page

PREPARE AHEAD: 1. In a bowl, cover the rice with cold water and soak for 2 hours. Then pour enough boiling water into the lower part of a steamer to come within an inch of the cooking rack (or use a steamer substitute as described on page 8). Line the rack with a double thickness of paper towels. Now drain the rice and spread it evenly over the lined rack. Over high heat, bring the water in the steamer to a rolling boil. Cover the pan tightly and steam the rice for 30 minutes, or until the rice is tender. Keep a kettle of boiling water on the stove to replenish the water in the steamer if necessary. Remove the rice from the pot, place it in a bowl and cover it with aluminum foil to keep warm.

2. In a small bowl, cover the dried shrimp with ¼ cup of warm water and allow them to soak for at least 30 minutes. Do not drain the shrimp or discard the water.

3. In a small bowl, cover the mushrooms with ½ cup of warm water and let them soak for at least 30 minutes. Then remove them with a slotted spoon and discard the water. With a cleaver or large, sharp knife, cut away and discard the tough stems of the mushrooms and chop the caps fine.

4. Meanwhile, bone the duck, following the directions and diagrams on pages 94 and 95.

5. Have the above ingredients, and the oil, pork, sugar, wine, soy sauce, gingko nuts, water chestnuts, ham, salt and parsley sprigs—plus trussing pins or clips or a large needle and strong thread for closing the cavities of the duck—within easy reach.

TO COOK: Set a 12-inch wok or 10-inch skillet over high heat for 30 seconds. Pour in the 2 tablespoons of oil, swirl it about in the pan and heat for another 30 seconds, turning the heat down to moderate if the oil begins to smoke. Add the pork and stir-fry for 2 or 3 minutes until the pork loses its reddish color. Stir in the wine and soy sauce, then add the mushrooms, gingko nuts, water chestnuts, rice, ham, shrimp and soaking water. Mix them together thoroughly and gently fold in the chestnuts, being careful not to let the chestnuts crumble. Transfer the entire contents of this stuffing mixture from the pan to a bowl and cool to room temperature.

Preheat the oven to 400°. Rub the inside surfaces of the duck with the 2 teaspoons of salt, then—with clips, trussing pins or needle and strong thread—close up the neck opening very securely. Pack the stuffing loosely into the cavity of the duck and close up the tail opening in exactly the same fashion as you already closed the neck. Pat, shape and mold the body of the duck back into its original shape and place it, breast side up, on a rack set in a deep roasting pan. Add about 1 inch of water to the pan. Roast in the center of the oven for 30 minutes, reduce the heat to 350° and roast the duck for 1½ hours longer.

When the duck is done, remove its clips, trussing pins or thread. Place the duck on a heated serving platter. Decorate the platter with fresh parsley sprigs and serve at once. At the table, carve the duck into 8 portions by first cutting it in half lengthwise and then making 3 evenly spaced crosswise cuts.

Cha-pai-kê
FRIED SQUABS

炸 白 鴿

2 squabs, approximately 12 ounces to 1 pound each
2 quarts cold water
1 scallion, including the green top, cut into 2-inch lengths
3 slices peeled fresh ginger root, about 1 inch in diameter and ⅛ inch thick
2 cups master sauce, prepared according to the recipe for braised soy sauce chicken on page 81
3 cups peanut oil, or flavorless vegetable oil
1 lemon, cut in quarters, or roasted salt and pepper prepared according to the recipe on page 93

PREPARE AHEAD: 1. With a cleaver, sharp, heavy knife or poultry shears, cut the squabs open along their backbones and spread them out. Place the birds, skin side down, on a chopping board, and, with the flat of the cleaver or a kitchen mallet, give them a few sharp blows to break their breastbones and flatten them. Wash the squabs quickly under cold running water and pat them dry with paper towels.

2. Have the squabs, water, scallions, ginger, master sauce and oil within easy reach.

TO COOK: Over high heat, bring the 2 quarts of water to a rolling boil in a 4-quart pot. Drop in the squabs, cover the pan tightly and turn off the heat. Let the squabs rest in the water for 5 minutes, then remove them and drain them on a double thickness of paper towels. Pour off the water from the pot and replace it with the master sauce. Add the squabs, bring the sauce to a boil and cover the pot. Reduce the heat to its lowest point and simmer undisturbed for 15 minutes, then remove the squabs and save the master sauce to be used again.

Pour 3 cups of oil into a 12-inch wok or deep-fryer and heat the oil until a haze forms above it or it registers 375° on a deep-frying thermometer. Drop in the scallions, ginger and squabs, and deep-fry for 2 or 3 minutes, turning them over with a large slotted spoon from time to time until the squabs are a golden brown all over. Remove them from the oil and drain on paper towels. Cut each squab into 6 pieces by just splitting it lengthwise along the breastbone and then chopping each half crosswise into 3 slices. Arrange the pieces—reconstructed in their original shapes—on a heated platter and serve at once with lemon quarters or with roasted salt and pepper. As a main course, this will serve 2. As part of a Chinese meal *(page 120)*, it will serve 4 to 6.

Pei-ching-k'ao-ya

PEKING DUCK

A 5-pound duck
6 cups water
¼ cup honey
4 slices peeled fresh ginger root,
    about 1 inch in diameter and ⅛
    inch thick
2 scallions, including the green tops,
    cut into 2-inch lengths

THE SAUCE

¼ cup *hoisin* sauce
1 tablespoon water
1 teaspoon sesame-seed oil
2 teaspoons sugar

12 scallions
Mandarin pancakes, prepared
    according to the recipe opposite
    and reheated

PREPARE AHEAD: 1. Wash the duck under cold water, then pat dry inside and out with paper towels. Tie one end of a 20-inch length of white cord around the neck skin. If the skin has been cut away, loop the cord under the wings. Suspend the bird from the string in a cool, airy place for 3 hours to dry the skin, or train a fan on it for 2 hours.

2. In a 12-inch wok or large flameproof casserole, combine 6 cups water, ¼ cup honey, ginger root and cut scallions, and bring to a boil over high heat. Holding the duck by its string, lower it into the boiling liquid. With string in one hand and a spoon in the other, turn the duck from side to side until all of its skin is moistened with the liquid. Remove the duck (discarding the liquid) and hang it again in the cool place, setting a bowl beneath it to catch any drippings; the duck will dry in 1 hour with the fan trained upon it or 2 to 3 hours without it.

3. Make the sauce by combining *hoisin* sauce, water, sesame-seed oil and sugar in a small pan, and stirring until sugar dissolves. Bring to a boil, then reduce heat to its lowest point and simmer uncovered for 3 minutes. Pour into a small bowl, cool and reserve until ready to use.

4. To make scallion brushes, cut scallions down to 3-inch lengths and trim off roots. Standing each scallion on end, make four intersecting cuts 1 inch deep into its stalk. Repeat at other end. Place scallions in ice water and refrigerate until cut parts curl into brushlike fans.

TO COOK: Preheat oven to 375°. Untie the duck and cut off any loose neck skin. Place duck, breast side up, on a rack and set in a roasting pan just large enough to hold the bird. Roast the duck in the middle of the oven for one hour. Then lower the heat to 300°, turn the duck on its breast and roast for 30 minutes longer. Now raise the heat to 375°, return the duck to its original position and roast for a final half hour. Transfer the duck to a carving board.

With a small, sharp knife and your fingers, remove the crisp skin from the breast, sides and back of duck. Cut skin into 2-by-3-inch rectangles and arrange them in a single layer on a heated platter. Cut the wings and drumsticks from the duck, and cut all the meat away from breast and carcass. Slice meat into pieces 2½ inches long and ½ inch wide, and arrange them with the wings and drumsticks on another heated platter.

To serve, place the platters of duck, the heated pancakes, the bowl of sauce and the scallion brushes in the center of the table. Traditionally, each guest spreads a pancake flat on his plate, dips a scallion in the sauce and brushes the pancake with it. The scallion is placed in the middle of the pancake with a piece of duck skin and a piece of meat on top. The pancake is folded over the scallion and duck, and tucked under. One end of the package is then folded over about 1 inch to enclose the filling, and the whole rolled into a cylinder that can be picked up with the fingers and eaten. As a main course, Peking duck will serve 6. As part of a Chinese meal *(page 120)*, it will serve 8 to 12. If you plan to serve more than 6, increase the number of pancakes and scallion brushes.

Po-ping
MANDARIN PANCAKES

薄餅

To make 2 dozen pancakes

3/4 cup boiling water

2 cups sifted all-purpose flour

1 to 2 tablespoons sesame-seed oil

Sift flour into a mixing bowl, make a well in the center and pour into it the 3/4 cup of boiling water. With a wooden spoon, gradually mix flour and water together until a soft dough is formed; on a lightly floured surface, knead it gently for 10 minutes, or until smooth and elastic. Cover with a damp kitchen towel and let it rest for 15 minutes. On a lightly floured surface, roll dough into a circle about 1/4 inch thick. With a 2 1/2-inch cookie cutter or a glass, cut as many circles of dough as you can. Knead scraps together, roll out again and cut more circles. Arrange circles side by side, brush half of them lightly with sesame-seed oil and, sandwich-wise, place the unoiled ones on top. With a rolling pin, flatten each pair into a 6-inch circle, rotating the sandwich an inch or so in a clockwise direction as you roll so that the circle keeps its shape, and turning it once to roll both sides. Cover the pancakes with a dry towel.

Set a heavy 8-inch skillet over high heat for 30 seconds. Reduce heat to moderate and cook the pancakes, one at a time, in the ungreased pan, turning them over as they puff up and little bubbles appear on the surface. Regulate the heat so that the pancakes become specked with brown after cooking about 1 minute on each side. As each pancake is finished, gently separate the halves and stack them on a plate. Serve them at once or wrap them in foil and refrigerate for later use. Or they may be wrapped and frozen, if you like. Reheat them (frozen pancakes need not be defrosted first) either by steaming them in a steamer for 10 minutes, or warming them, still wrapped in their foil, in a preheated 350° oven for about 10 minutes. Serve with Peking duck *(opposite)* and soft-fried shredded pork and eggs *(page 66)*.

Hao-yu-kê-sung

蠔油鴿鬆

MINCED SQUAB WITH OYSTER SAUCE

6 dried oysters

4 dried Chinese mushrooms, 1 to 1½
inches in diameter

¼ cup shelled fresh peas or
thoroughly defrosted frozen peas

2 squabs, about 12 ounces each, or
substitute ½ pound fresh ground
pork combined with ½ pound
boneless skinned chicken meat

1 head of lettuce, preferably Bibb or
Boston

2 tablespoons peanut oil, or flavorless
vegetable oil

1 scallion, including the green top,
finely chopped

½ teaspoon finely chopped, peeled
fresh ginger root

¼ cup coarsely chopped canned water
chestnuts

1 tablespoon soy sauce

2 tablespoons oyster sauce

¼ teaspoon sugar

1 teaspoon cornstarch dissolved in 1
tablespoon cold chicken stock,
fresh or canned, or cold water

PREPARE AHEAD: 1. In a small bowl, cover the dried oysters with ½ cup of warm water and let them soak for 30 minutes. Drain and discard the water. Chop the oysters fine.

2. In another small bowl, cover the mushrooms with ½ cup of warm water and let them soak for 30 minutes. Then remove them with a slotted spoon, strain the soaking water through a fine sieve and reserve 2 tablespoons of it. With a cleaver or sharp knife, cut away and discard the tough stems of the mushrooms, and chop the caps fine.

3. Blanch the freshly shelled peas by dropping them into 2 cups of rapidly boiling water and letting them boil uncovered for 5 to 10 minutes, or until tender. Then drain and run cold water over them to stop their cooking and set their color. Frozen peas need only be thoroughly defrosted.

4. With a cleaver or sharp knife, skin the squabs. Cut the meat from the bones and discard the bones. Then finely chop the meat. If you are substituting pork and chicken for the squabs, chop the chicken meat fine and mix it thoroughly with the ground pork.

5. Separate the lettuce leaves, wash and pat them dry with paper towels. Cut them into 5-inch rounds. Arrange the rounds on a serving plate and refrigerate.

6. Have the oysters, mushrooms, peas, squabs (or their substitute), and the oil, scallions, ginger, water chestnuts, soy sauce, oyster sauce, sugar and cornstarch mixture within easy reach.

TO COOK: Set a 12-inch wok or 10-inch skillet over high heat for 30 seconds. Pour in the 2 tablespoons of oil, swirl it about in the pan and heat for another 30 seconds, turning the heat down to moderate if the oil begins to smoke. Immediately add the scallions and ginger, cook for a few seconds, then drop in the squab and stir-fry for 1 minute. (If substituting the pork and chicken mixture, stir-fry for 2 or 3 minutes.) Add the soy sauce, sugar, oyster sauce, and then the oysters, mushrooms and water chestnuts. Stir once again and drop in the peas. Then add the mushroom water, stir and cook 1 minute. Give the cornstarch mixture a stir to re-combine it and add it to the pan. Stir constantly until all the ingredients are coated with a light, clear glaze. Transfer the entire contents of the pan to a platter and serve at once accompanied by the lettuce leaves.

Traditionally, each guest spreads a lettuce leaf flat on his plate and places about 2 tablespoonfuls of the squab mixture in the middle of the leaf. The leaf is folded in half over the minced squab and tucked gently under it; one end of the package is then folded over about 1 inch to en-close the filling securely, and the whole rolled into a neat cylinder that can be picked up with the fingers and eaten.

As a main course, this will serve 2 to 4. As part of a Chinese meal *(page 120)*, it will serve 4 to 6.

H'sün-tan 燻蛋

SMOKED EGGS

6 eggs	½ teaspoon bottled liquid smoke
2 tablespoons soy sauce	1 teaspoon sugar
1 teaspoon sesame-seed oil	½ teaspoon salt

TO COOK: In a 1½- to 2-quart saucepan, cover the eggs with 2 cups of cold water, bring to a boil over high heat, reduce the heat and simmer uncovered for 4 minutes. Remove the eggs with a slotted spoon, plunge them immediately into a bowl of cold water and let them remain there for at least 5 minutes. This will stop their cooking and keep the yolks somewhat soft, as they should be. Carefully shell the eggs and place them side by side in a shallow dish just large enough to hold them in one layer. In a small bowl combine the soy sauce, sesame-seed oil, liquid smoke, sugar and salt. Pour the mixture over the eggs and let them marinate at room temperature for 2 to 3 hours, turning them over every 30 minutes to keep them well moistened with the marinade.

TO SERVE: Just before serving, cut the eggs in half and arrange them on an attractive plate. Smoked eggs may be served separately as an hors d'oeuvre, or they may be part of a Chinese cold plate served with various meats and salads.

Hsia-jen-ch'ao-tan

蝦仁炒蛋

SHRIMP EGG FOO YUNG

To serve 6

½ cup fresh or canned bean sprouts
3 to 4 medium fresh mushrooms, cut
   into ¼-inch dice (about ½ cup)
½ pound raw shrimp in their shells
¼ cup peanut oil, or flavorless
   vegetable oil
3 eggs

FOO YUNG SAUCE
¾ cup chicken stock, fresh or canned
1 tablespoon soy sauce
½ teaspoon salt
1 tablespoon cornstarch dissolved in
   2 tablespoons cold chicken stock,
   fresh or canned, or cold water

PREPARE AHEAD: 1. Rinse fresh bean sprouts in a pot of cold water and discard any husks that float to the surface. Drain and pat them dry. To crisp canned sprouts, rinse them under running water and refrigerate them in a bowl of cold water for 2 hours. Drain and pat them dry.

2. Shell the shrimp. With a small, sharp knife, make a shallow incision down their backs and lift out the intestinal vein. Wash the shrimp under cold water, pat them dry and cut them into ¼-inch dice.

3. Have the bean sprouts, shrimp, mushrooms, eggs and oil, and the stock, soy sauce, salt and cornstarch mixture within easy reach.

TO COOK: In a small saucepan, bring the stock to a boil. Add the soy sauce, salt and cornstarch mixture. Reduce the heat and cook for 2 minutes until the sauce is thick and clear. Keep warm over low heat.

Set a 12-inch wok or 8-inch skillet over high heat for 30 seconds. Pour in 1 tablespoon of oil, swirl it about and heat for another 30 seconds, turning the heat down if the oil begins to smoke. Add the shrimp and stir-fry for 1 minute, or until they are firm and light pink. Transfer them to a plate. Break the eggs into a bowl and beat them with a fork or whisk until they are well combined. Add the shrimp, bean sprouts and mushrooms. Set the wok or skillet again over high heat for 30 seconds. Add 1 tablespoon oil, swirl it about, reduce the heat to low, then pour in about ¼ cup of the egg mixture. Let it cook undisturbed for 1 minute, or until lightly browned. Turn the pancake over and cook for another minute. Transfer the pancake to a heatproof platter and cover with foil to keep warm.

Following the same procedure, make 5 more pancakes with the remaining egg mixture. Add about 1 teaspoon of oil to the wok or skillet for each new pancake and stack them on the platter as you proceed. Serve with sauce poured over each pancake. Although it is not classic, some Chinese cooks garnish this dish with green peas.

ROAST PORK EGG FOO YUNG: Substitute ½ cup of diced roast pork for the cooked shrimp, but otherwise follow this recipe precisely.

Tan-chuan

蛋 捲

ROLLED EGG PANCAKE WITH PORK FILLING

To make about 16 slices

THE FILLING
½ pound boneless pork shoulder, finely ground
2 teaspoons soy sauce
1 teaspoon cornstarch
1 tablespoon Chinese rice wine, or pale dry sherry

1 teaspoon salt
1 egg, lightly beaten

THE EGG PANCAKES
4 eggs
2 teaspoons peanut oil, or flavorless vegetable oil

PREPARE AHEAD: 1. In a small bowl, combine the pork, soy sauce, cornstarch, wine, salt and beaten egg, and mix them thoroughly together.

2. Beat the 4 eggs with a fork or whisk just enough to combine them.

3. Have the pork mixture, beaten eggs and oil within easy reach.

TO COOK: Set a 12-inch wok or 8-inch skillet over moderate heat for about 30 seconds. With a pastry brush or paper towel, brush the bottom of the pan with 1 teaspoon of oil. Pour in half the beaten eggs. Lower the heat at once and—working quickly but carefully—tip the pan from side to side until a thin, round pancake about 8 inches in diameter forms. Immediately pour any uncooked egg on the surface of the pancake back into the bowl. As soon as the pancake is firm enough to handle—no more than 30 seconds—lift it up with your fingers or a spatula and transfer it to a plate. In similar fashion, make another pancake, transferring it to a second plate when it is done. Reserve any uncooked egg. Spread half of the pork filling over each pancake. Roll them tightly, jelly-roll fashion, and seal the edges with a little reserved uncooked egg. Press the edges together firmly to make them adhere.

Pour boiling water into the steamer to come within an inch of the rack (or use a steamer substitute, page 8). Lay the pancakes on a heatproof platter ½ inch smaller than the diameter of the pot. Set this on the rack; cover the pot. Keeping the water at a slow boil, steam the pancakes for 20 minutes. Remove the platter from the steamer. Cut the rolls diagonally into ½-inch slices and serve hot. Or refrigerate the whole rolls, and serve them cold. (Peas may be used as garnish, but are not classic.)

Desserts

Tsao-ni-hün-tün

棗泥餛飩

DEEP-FRIED WONTONS WITH DATE FILLING

To make about 4 dozen

One recipe *wonton* wrappers *(page 3)*, or 1 pound ready-made egg-roll wrappers, cut into quarters

THE FILLING

4 eight-ounce packages pitted dates

2 cups finely chopped walnuts

3 tablespoons grated fresh orange rind

3 to 5 tablespoons orange juice or cold water (if needed)

3 cups peanut oil, or flavorless vegetable oil

Confectioners' sugar

PREPARE AHEAD: 1. To make the filling: With a cleaver or sharp knife, chop the pitted dates fine, adding a teaspoon or so of orange juice or water if they are too sticky to cut. Combine the dates, walnuts and grated rind in a small bowl. Knead the mixture with your fingers until it can be gathered into a ball. If the mixture is dry, moisten it with orange juice or water. Roll a tablespoon of filling between the palms of your hands to form cylinders 1 inch long and about ⅓ inch in diameter.

2. To assemble the *wontons:* Place a cylinder of filling diagonally across each wrapper, just below the center. With a finger dipped in water, moisten the lower point of the wrapper. Fold the point over the filling and tuck it underneath. Roll up the resulting tube until all the dough surrounds the filling. Stick a finger into each end of the tube and give it a twist to seal the ends.

TO COOK: Pour the oil into a 12-inch wok or deep-fryer and heat the oil until a haze forms above it or it reaches 375° on a deep-frying thermometer. Deep-fry the *wontons*, 8 or 10 at a time, turning them occasionally, for 2 to 3 minutes, or until they are golden brown and crisp. As they are finished cooking, transfer them to paper towels to drain and cool. Just before serving, sprinkle the *wontons* with confectioners' sugar.

Pa-ssŭ-ping-kuo

拔絲蘋果

SPUN APPLES

To make 16 spun apple slices

1 cup all-purpose flour
1 egg, lightly beaten and combined
   with ½ cup plus 2 tablespoons of
   cold water

2 medium-sized firm apples
3 cups plus 1 tablespoon peanut oil,
   or flavorless vegetable oil
1 cup sugar
¼ cup cold water
1 tablespoon black sesame seeds

PREPARE AHEAD: Pour the 1 cup of flour into a good-sized bowl and then, little by little, pour the beaten egg and water mixture into the flour, stirring constantly with a large spoon. Stir until you have formed a fairly smooth batter.

2. With a small, sharp knife, cut the apples into quarters. Peel off the skin and cut away the cores. Then cut the quarters into eighths.

3. Arrange your ingredients—the batter, the apples, the oil, the sugar, the water and the sesame seeds—within easy reach and set out a large serving plate lightly greased with oil and a large bowl containing one quart of water plus a dozen ice cubes.

TO COOK: In a 2- to 3-quart saucepan, heat the 3 cups of oil until a haze forms above it or it reaches a temperature of 375° on a deep-frying thermometer. At the same time, in a 12-inch wok or 10-inch skillet, heat the 1 tablespoon of oil with the sugar and water. Bring the sugar and water to a boil over high heat, stirring only until the sugar dissolves. Cook this mixture briskly without stirring until the syrup registers 300° on a candy thermometer or reaches the hard crack stage; that is to say, when a very small amount of the syrup dropped into ice water instantly forms a hard mass. Stir in the black sesame seeds and turn the heat down to its lowest point.

Now proceed to make the spun apples in the following fashion: Drop 8 of the apple wedges into the batter, stirring them about to coat them thoroughly. With chopsticks, tongs or a slotted spoon, transfer the wedges to the heated oil and deep-fry them for 1 minute, or until they turn light amber. Immediately, lift them out of the oil and put them into the skillet of hot syrup. Stir the wedges to coat them thoroughly with syrup, then—still using chopsticks, tongs or a slotted spoon—drop them one at a time into the bowl of ice water. The syrup coating will harden instantly and enclose each piece of apple in a clear, brilliant glaze. Transfer the finished spun apples to the lightly greased serving plate and make the second batch in precisely the same manner. Serve the spun apples as soon as you possibly can. The delicate candy glaze will soften if they are allowed to stand for long.

Li-tzŭ-tan-kao

栗 子 蛋 糕

PEKING DUST

To serve 6 to 8

1 cup shelled pecans	1 pound fresh chestnuts
½ cup white sugar	2 tablespoons brown sugar
1 cup peanut oil, or flavorless	½ cup water
vegetable oil	½ pint heavy cream
	2 tablespoons white sugar

PREPARE AHEAD: 1. In a small saucepan, combine the pecans with 2 cups of water. Bring to a boil over high heat, reduce the heat to moderate and simmer uncovered for 1 minute. Remove the pan from the heat and pour off all the water. Add the ½ cup of sugar and stir until the pecans are evenly coated. With a spoon, spread the pecans out on a sheet of wax paper and let them dry for 30 minutes. Set a 12-inch wok or 10-inch skillet over high heat and pour in 1 cup of oil. Heat the oil until a haze forms above it or it registers 375° on a deep-frying thermometer. Fry the pecans for 1 or 2 minutes, turning and separating them with a slotted spoon until the sugar coats the nuts with a rich brown glaze. Transfer the nuts to a large greased platter and spread them apart in a single layer to cool to room temperature.

2. Shell the chestnuts in the following fashion: Preheat the oven to 425°. With a small, sharp knife, cut a crisscross on the top of each chestnut. Spread the nuts out in a single layer in a shallow baking pan and pour in about ¼ cup of water—just enough to film the bottom of the pan. Roast the chestnuts for 10 minutes, or until they pop open. Turn off the oven and remove half the nuts from the pan. While the chestnuts are still hot, remove their shells and inner brown membranes with a small, sharp knife. Then peel the hot chestnuts similarly.

TO ASSEMBLE: In a heavy 3-quart saucepan, combine the brown sugar and ½ cup cold water. Add the shelled chestnuts, and turn them about with a spoon to coat them evenly with the sugar and water. Bring to a simmer over moderate heat, cover the pan and reduce the heat to the lowest possible point. Cook the chestnuts undisturbed for 45 minutes, or until tender; the liquid will cook away, leaving them quite dry. Uncover the pan, turn off the heat and let the chestnuts cool to room temperature.

Purée the chestnuts in a food mill set over a mixing bowl. If the purée seems coarse—it should be as fine as granulated sugar—press it through the mill a second time. With a whisk, or rotary or electric beater, whip the cream and remaining white sugar in a large bowl until the cream is stiff enough to form firm unwavering peaks when the whisk or beater is lifted out of the bowl. Spoon the whipped cream into a cone-shaped mound on a chilled serving platter. A few tablespoons at a time, sprinkle the chestnut purée over the cream, masking it completely. Arrange the glazed pecans side by side in a ring around the edge of the platter. Serve the finished dessert at once.

Hsing-jen-tou-fu　　　　　　　　杏仁豆腐
ALMOND FLOAT

This is a modernized version of a classic Chinese dish. The original recipe did not, of course, use gelatin or almond extract. The jelling agent in the original version was agar-agar, a type of seaweed, which was boiled until it dissolved, producing a clear, flavorless aspic; because agar-agar produces jellies of varying consistencies it is difficult to use with any precision. Instead of almond extract, the ancient Chinese crushed whole almonds, soaked them in water and squeezed out the liquid. Commercial almond extract produces comparable results.

To serve 6 to 8

2 packages unflavored gelatin	½ cup sugar
1¾ cups cold water	
1½ cups milk	GARNISH
1 tablespoon almond extract	A 6½-ounce can mandarin orange sections
SYRUP	A 1-pound can litchi nuts
2 cups cold water	

PREPARE AHEAD: 1. In a large heatproof bowl, sprinkle the gelatin over ½ cup of cold water and let it soften for 5 minutes.

2. Bring the remaining 1¼ cups of water to a boil in a small saucepan and add it to the softened gelatin. Stir until it has thoroughly dissolved and become clear, then stir in the milk and almond extract. Pour the mixture into a flat 7½-by-12-inch dish. The custard should be about 1½ inch thick. Refrigerate for at least 3 to 4 hours, or until the custard is firmly set.

3. Make the syrup meanwhile by combining 2 cups of water with ½ cup of sugar in a small saucepan. Bring to a boil and cool, then chill in the refrigerator. The syrup will be properly thin as it should be.

TO ASSEMBLE: With a sharp knife, make diagonal cuts 1 inch apart in the almond float. Repeat in the opposite direction to form diamond-shaped pieces. Carefully lift the diamonds out of the dish with a small spatula and arrange them with the orange sections and litchi nuts in several layers in a deep serving bowl. Pour on the chilled syrup and serve.

Pa-pao-fan

八寶飯

EIGHT-TREASURE RICE PUDDING

*This dessert is known as eight-treasure or eight-precious or even eight-jewel pud-
ding because in China the design on the top of it was made with 8 different kinds
of dried and candied fruits or nuts—such as dried lotus seeds, candied green or
red plums, seeded dragon's eye nuts, watermelon seeds, preserved dates, dried jujubes, candied orange peel, candied red or green cherries, and blanched walnuts.
The version described here is simply decorated with pitted dates, dried jujubes and
candied cherries.*

To serve 8

2 cups glutinous rice
¼ cup lard
½ pound pitted dates, finely
    chopped, plus 8 whole pitted dates,
    cut in half
1 cup canned red-bean paste
20 dried jujubes
2 tablespoons sugar

2 tablespoons melted lard
Red and green candied cherries

SYRUP
¼ cup sugar
1 cup cold water
1 teaspoon almond extract
1 tablespoon cornstarch dissolved in
    3 tablespoons cold water

PREPARE AHEAD: 1. In a large bowl, cover the rice with cold water and
soak for 2 hours.

2. In a 12-inch wok or 10-inch skillet, melt the ¼ cup of lard over moderate heat. Add the chopped dates and red-bean paste, and cook over low
heat, stirring frequently, for 20 minutes, or until the mixture begins to
come away from the sides of the pan. Remove from the pan to a small
bowl and cool to room temperature.

3. Combine the jujubes and 2 cups cold water in a 2-quart saucepan.
Over high heat, bring the water to a boil, then reduce the heat to low
and simmer the jujubes, covered, for about 10 minutes. Drain the jujubes
through a sieve, and, when they are cool enough to handle, cut them in
half and remove and discard the pits.

4. Have the rice, date and bean-paste mixture, jujubes, cherries, sugar,
water, almond extract and cornstarch all within easy reach.

TO COOK: Pour enough boiling water into the lower part of a steamer
to come within an inch of the cooking rack (or use a steamer substitute
as described on page 8). Line the rack with a double layer of paper towels. Drain the rice and spread it evenly over the lined rack. Over high
heat, bring the water in the steamer to a rolling boil, cover the pan tightly and steam the rice for 30 minutes, or until the rice is thoroughly
cooked, replenishing the water if it boils away.

Transfer the rice to a bowl, and stir into it the 2 tablespoons of sugar
and 2 tablespoons of melted lard. Spoon half the rice into a shallow heat-

proof bowl (about 6 inches across and 3 inches deep). On top, place the red-bean-paste mixture, spreading it to within ½ inch of the sides of the bowl. Place the remaining rice over it, spreading it out evenly to the edges of the bowl and pressing down on it lightly with the palm of your hand. Put an inverted dinner plate over the top of the bowl, and, grasping the edges of both the plate and the bowl, turn them over together. Lift the bowl up gently to unmold the pudding. Now decorate the sides and top of the pudding with the jujubes, halved dates and candied cherries. Any sort of design you devise would be proper. For instance, the bottom edge of the pudding may be decorated with a row of date halves spaced about an inch apart, the top edge rimmed with jujubes, laid side by side, and the top of the pudding ornamented with flowers and leaves made of cherries.

When the decoration is complete, gently spread a long piece of plastic wrap over it to hold the fruit in place, invert the bowl again and carefully set it over the top of the pudding. Grasping the edges of the bowl and plate together, turn the bowl over and remove the plate. Bring the water in the steamer to a boil again, place the bowl on the rack and cover the pan tightly. Steam the pudding for an hour, replenishing the water when it boils away. Have a kettle of boiling water handy.

TO SERVE: A few minutes before the pudding is done, make the syrup by combining the ¼ cup of sugar with the cup of water in a small saucepan and boiling it until the sugar dissolves. Add the almond extract, give the cornstarch mixture a quick stir to recombine it and stir it into the syrup. Cook, stirring, for a few seconds until the syrup thickens slightly and becomes clear. Now remove the pudding from the steamer and place a circular serving plate over it. Grasping bowl and plate securely, turn them over. The pudding should slide out easily. Carefully peel off the plastic wrap. Pour the hot syrup over the pudding and serve at once.

Hsi-mi-chü-keng
西米橘羹

HOT ORANGE PUDDING

To serve 4 to 6

½ cup pearl tapioca
1 large orange

2½ cups cold water
¼ cup sugar

PREPARE AHEAD: 1. In a small bowl, cover the tapioca with ½ cup of cold water and let it soak for at least 4 hours.

2. With a small knife, peel the orange and remove the white membrane clinging to each section. Break the orange meat into small pieces.

3. Have the tapioca, orange and sugar within easy reach.

TO COOK: In a 2-quart saucepan, combine 2 cups of cold water with the sugar. Bring to a boil over high heat, stirring until the sugar dissolves. Drain the tapioca and pour it into the pan slowly, stirring constantly. Cook over moderate heat, stirring, for 2 minutes until the pudding thickens. Stir in the orange and bring to a boil again. Serve at once.

Shih-chin-kuo-pin
什錦菓品

WATERMELON SHELLS FILLED WITH FRUIT

To serve 6 to 8

1 medium-sized, firm ripe watermelon
  (about 10 pounds)
24 canned litchis, drained

8 canned loquats, drained
8 preserved kumquats, drained
8 canned water-pack kumquats,
  drained

Using a cleaver or large, sharp knife, cut the melon in half crosswise. Scoop out most of the melon pulp with a large spoon, leaving a shell of pulp about ½ inch thick inside each half. Carefully remove and discard all the watermelon seeds. If desired, cut a design in the outer rind with a sharp knife or scallop the top edges of each melon half.

Cut the melon pulp into 1-inch cubes or, with a melon baller, shape it into balls. In a large bowl, combine the melon cubes or balls with the litchis, loquats and kumquats. Spoon the fruit into the two melon shells, dividing the fruit evenly between them. Chill thoroughly before serving.

NOTE: Other fruits—such as cantaloupe or honeydew melon balls, orange sections or apple wedges—may be added to the mixture in the melon shells, or substituted for the fruits listed above if these are not readily available.

Hsing-jen-ping

杏仁餅

ALMOND COOKIES

To make 8 dozen cookies

½ pound lard
¾ cup sugar
2 eggs
1 tablespoon almond extract
4 drops yellow food coloring

2½ cups unsifted flour
½ teaspoon baking soda
¼ teaspoon salt
½ cup blanched almonds, split in
    half
1 egg, lightly beaten

PREPARE AHEAD: In a large mixing bowl, cream the lard and sugar by beating them together with a large spoon until light and fluffy. Beat in the eggs, one at a time, then add the almond extract and yellow food coloring. Combine the flour, baking soda and salt and sift them into the bowl. With your fingers, mix the ingredients together until a fairly firm dough is formed. Divide the dough in half and shape it into two fat cylinders, then roll them on a lightly floured surface with the palms of your hands until each cylinder is about 12 inches long and 1½ inches in diameter. Wrap in wax paper and refrigerate for at least 3 hours.

TO COOK: Preheat the oven to 375°. With a cleaver or sharp knife, cut the chilled dough crosswise into slices ¼ inch thick. Lay a dozen or so of the circles side by side and 1 inch apart on an ungreased cookie sheet, and press an almond half gently but firmly in the center of each. Brush the cookies with a thin film of beaten egg and bake in the center of the oven for about 10 minutes, or until they are golden brown. With a spatula, transfer the cookies to a rack to cool.

Chinese Tea

To serve 6

2 tablespoons black or green tea
    leaves

4 cups water

Scald the inside of a glass or china teapot with boiling water, drain and then add the tea leaves. Bring the 4 cups of water to a full rolling boil in a kettle or saucepan and pour it into the teapot. The leaves should rise to the top of the pot, then sink slowly to the bottom. (If the water is not at a full boil when it is poured into the teapot, some leaves will remain on the top and the flavor of the finished tea will be flat or bitter.) Let the tea steep covered and undisturbed for 3 to 5 minutes, depending on the strength desired.

Recipe Index:

Hors d'Oeuvre and Dim Sum

Soups and Fire Pots

Vegetables and Salads

Noodles and Rice

Fish and Seafood

Meat

Poultry and Eggs

Desserts

A Guide to Ingredients in Chinese Cooking

Most of the ingredients called for in this book's recipes can be found at any grocery store or supermarket. The less common ingredients, which are listed and described on these pages, may require a visit to a specialty store. Some Chinese foods can be approximated by more familiar ingredients — but substitutes often change the character of a dish somewhat. If an ingredient is not available, the best course is often to omit it from the recipe. To make your shopping easier, the name of each food is shown in Chinese characters above its English name. Many Chinese markets do their own packaging, usually in small plastic bags to encourage experimentation. By shopping around, one can find a large selection packaged in various sizes.

罐 頭 筍

BAMBOO SHOOTS: Ivory-colored, conical-shaped shoots of tropical bamboo, usually about 3 inches across and 4 inches long. Sold canned in Oriental specialty stores. (Can sizes range from 4 ounces up.) Large wedges packed in water are best. After opening, drain and store in fresh water in a covered jar in the refrigerator, changing the water daily. Can be kept for about 10 days. Kohlrabi or celery hearts are similar in texture but not flavor.

豆 腐

BEAN CURD, FRESH: Square, custardlike cakes of pressed pureed soybeans. Sold by the cake, usually ½ to ¾ inch thick and 3 inches square, in Oriental specialty stores, health food stores and many supermarkets. Drain and store in fresh water in a covered jar in the refrigerator for up to 2 weeks, changing the water daily. No substitute.

二 竹

BEAN-CURD SKIN: Thin, stiff sheets of dried bean curd. Sold by weight in Chinese specialty stores (5 to 6 sheets weigh about 1 ounce). Needs no refrigeration. No substitute.

綠 豆 芽

BEAN SPROUTS: Young sprouts of the mung bean, 1½ to 2 inches long. Sold fresh by weight and in 4- to 8-ounce cans. The fresh ones have parchmentlike husks that must be removed before using. Refrigerate fresh sprouts in water in a covered jar for up to 2 weeks. After opening canned sprouts, drain and store in fresh water in a covered jar in the refrigerator — they will keep for 2 to 3 days. No substitute.

燕 窩

BIRD'S NEST: Fragments of a translucent, gelatinous material with which Asian swiftlets coat their nests. Available in Chinese specialty stores, usually in 4- to 8-ounce packages. Needs no refrigeration. No substitute.

豆 豉

BLACK BEANS, FERMENTED: Strongly flavored, preserved black soybeans. Sold in 3- to 4-ounce cans and 3- to 4-ounce plastic bags in Chinese specialty shops. After opening, store up to 6 months, refrigerated, in tightly covered container or plastic bag. Add a few drops of peanut oil or flavorless vegetable oil or water if they seem to be drying out. Substitute extra soy sauce or salt.

白 菜

BOK CHOY: A variety of Chinese cabbage that grows somewhat like celery but has 12- to 16-inch-long smooth white stalks and large dark-green leaves. Sold fresh by the bunch or weight in Oriental specialty stores and some vegetable stores and supermarkets. Refrigerate in plastic bag for about a week. Substitute celery cabbage or romaine lettuce.

原 晒 豉

BROWN-BEAN SAUCE: Thick sauce made from fermented yellow beans, flour and salt. Sold in cans of 1 pound or more in Chinese specialty stores. After opening, it keeps for months refrigerated in a covered jar. Substitute additional salt.

天 津 白 菜

CELERY CABBAGE: A variety of Chinese cabbage that grows like celery but has crisp, tightly packed, yellow-white stalks 14 to 16 inches long and 4 to 5 inches wide. Sold fresh by the bunch or weight in Oriental specialty stores and some vegetable stores and supermarkets. Store, refrigerated, for about 2 weeks. Substitute savoy cabbage.

粉 絲

CELLOPHANE NOODLES (BEAN THREAD): Thin, translucent noodles made from ground mung beans. Dried in looped skeins and sold in 2- to 6-ounce packages in Chinese specialty stores. Wrap to store. No substitute.

雲 耳

CLOUD EAR: Small, crinkly, gelatinous dried fungus, about 1 inch long. Sold by weight in Chinese specialty shops. Store in a covered jar. No substitute.

芫 茜

CORIANDER, FRESH (CHINESE PARSLEY OR CILANTRO): Aromatic herb with flat leaves and stronger flavor than curly parsley. Sold fresh by the bunch in Chinese, Italian and Latin American grocery stores and some vegetable stores. Store in plastic bag in refrigerator for a week. Substitute flat-leaf Italian parsley for appearance but not flavor.

蘇 梅 醬

DUCK SAUCE (PLUM SAUCE): Reddish-brown condiment with sweet and pungent flavor made from plums, apricots, chili, vinegar and sugar. Sold in 1-pound cans and 4- to 12-ounce bottles in Chinese specialty stores and in gourmet shops. After opening, can be kept, refrigerated, for months. The canned variety should be transferred to a covered jar. No substitute.

蛋 麵

EGG NOODLES, CHINESE: Long, thin noodles no more than ⅛ inch wide made of flour, eggs and water. Sold, by the pound, fresh or dried, in Chinese specialty stores. Fresh ones may be stored in plastic bags in the freezer for months or in the refrigerator for 1 week. Substitute any other narrow egg noodle.

五 香 粉

FIVE-SPICE POWDER: A combination of five ground spices (anise seed, fennel, clove, cinnamon and Szechwan pepper) sold ready-mixed by weight in Chinese specialty stores. Store at room temperature in tightly covered container. Substitute allspice.

薑

GINGER ROOT, FRESH: Gnarled brown root, about 3 inches long. Sold by weight. Whole ginger root will keep for a few weeks wrapped in paper toweling in the refrigerator. Peeled, sliced fresh ginger root may be placed in a jar of dry sherry and refrigerated for several months. Peeled, sliced ginger root in brine is available in cans and may be substituted.

海 鮮 醬

HOISIN SAUCE: Sweet, brownish-red sauce made from soybeans, flour, sugar, water, spices, garlic and chili, for use in cooking. Sold in 1-pound cans and larger. After opening, can be stored for several months in the refrigerator in tightly covered container. No substitute.

白 蘿 蔔

ICICLE RADISH: White, crisp-textured radish about 2 to 4 inches in diameter and 6 to 10 inches long. Available only in Oriental specialty shops. Can be stored in vegetable section of refrigerator for about a week. Substitute the small white radishes sold in supermarkets and vegetable stores. These are sometimes also called icicle radishes but are not the same variety as the Chinese vegetable.

紅棗

JUJUBES (RED DATES): Small, red dried fruit with puckered skin and a sweet, subtle prunelike flavor. Sold by weight in Chinese specialty stores. Must be covered with boiling water and soaked 1 to 2 hours before using. Store in covered container. Substitute prunes, not California dates.

金橘

KUMQUATS: Yellow-orange citrus fruit, about 1 to 1½ inches long, with a tart orange flavor. Sometimes available fresh in midwinter or early spring, but usually sold in cans and jars of various sizes, often preserved in rich syrup. Found in Chinese specialty shops, gourmet food stores and many supermarkets. After opening canned kumquats, store in their own syrup in a tightly covered jar in the refrigerator. No substitute.

荔枝

LITCHIS: Small, oval fruit with rough red skin, white pulp and large pit. Sold fresh in July in Chinese specialty stores; or in 1-pound cans or dried in 10-ounce packets in Chinese stores and gourmet shops. After opening, refrigerate the canned variety in its own syrup in a tightly covered jar. No substitute.

枇杷

LOQUATS: Small, yellow-orange pitted fruit the size of an apricot with peach flavor. Sold pitted and preserved in 14-ounce cans in Chinese specialty stores. After opening, store in own syrup in a covered jar in the refrigerator. Substitute canned apricots or peaches.

藕

LOTUS ROOT: Long, potatolike root. Sold fresh in sections about 2 to 3 inches in diameter and 4 to 6 inches long, canned in various sizes, and dried in 4-ounce boxes in Chinese specialty stores. Each has a different texture and flavor, and they cannot be used interchangeably. Store the fresh or canned roots in the refrigerator. No substitute.

冬菇

MUSHROOMS, CHINESE DRIED: Strongly-flavored dried mushrooms from ¾ to 2 inches in diameter. Sold by weight or already packaged in Oriental specialty shops. Can be stored indefinitely, at room temperature in a covered jar. No substitute. (European dried mushrooms have a different taste.)

酸菜

MUSTARD GREENS, PICKLED: Green, cabbagelike vegetable packed in brine. Sold in 16-ounce jars, 16-ounce cans and from barrels in Chinese specialty stores. Store in the refrigerator. Substitute rinsed sauerkraut.

蠔油

OYSTER SAUCE: Thick, brown sauce with a rich flavor, made from oysters, soy sauce and brine. Sold in 6- or 12-ounce bottles in Oriental specialty shops. It will keep indefinitely. No substitute.

紅豆沙

RED-BEAN PASTE: Thick, sweet paste made from red soybeans. Available in cans in Oriental specialty shops. It will keep for months refrigerated in a covered jar. No substitute.

糯米

RICE, GLUTINOUS: A variety of short-grain rice which becomes sticky when cooked. Sold by weight in Chinese specialty stores. Store in a covered container. No substitute.

米粉

RICE STICK NOODLES: Thin, brittle white noodles, dried in 8-inch looped skeins. Sold in 8- to 16-ounce packages in Chinese specialty stores. Will keep indefinitely. No substitute.

鹹蛋

SALTED EGGS: Duck eggs soaked in brine for a month or more. Sold individually in Chinese specialty stores only. The yolks are sold separately in packets. Store in refrigerator. No substitute.

芝 蔴

SESAME SEEDS: Tiny, flat seeds, either black or white. Sold by weight in Oriental specialty stores, in Middle Eastern and Italian stores, and gourmet food shops. Store in a covered container. No substitute.

蔴 油

SESAME-SEED OIL: Strong, faintly nutty-flavored oil made from roasted sesame seeds. Sold in bottles in Oriental specialty stores. It will keep indefinitely. No substitute. Do not confuse it with the mild sesame-seed oil sold in some supermarkets.

魚 翅

SHARK'S FIN: Long threads of dried cartilage from the fins of sharks. Sold by weight and in 6- or 8-ounce boxes in Chinese specialty stores. It will keep indefinitely. No substitute.

蝦 米

SHRIMP, DRIED: Tiny shelled and dried shrimp with a sharp, salty flavor. Sold by weight in Chinese specialty shops. Store in a jar. No substitute.

大 腿

SMITHFIELD HAM: Cured smoked ham with a strong, distinctive flavor, sold already cooked. Not Chinese, but close in taste to Chinese ham. Available by weight or by the slice in Chinese specialty stores, gourmet shops and some supermarkets. Will keep for several weeks tightly wrapped in foil or plastic in refrigerator. Substitute Italian *prosciutto* or Westphalian ham.

雪 豆

SNOW PEAS: Flat, pale-green peas eaten pods and all. Sold fresh by weight in Oriental specialty stores and some vegetable stores and supermarkets; also available frozen in 10-ounce boxes in supermarkets. Store fresh ones in plastic bag in refrigerator; use as soon as possible.

醬 油

SOY SAUCE: Pungent, salty, brown liquid made from fermented soybeans, wheat, yeast and salt. The imported Chinese and Japanese sauces are best and are available in various-sized bottles in supermarkets as well as Oriental specialty stores.

八 角

STAR ANISE: Dry, brown, licorice-flavored spice that looks like an 8-pointed star about an inch across. Sold whole (though often the sections break apart) by weight in Chinese specialty stores. Store indefinitely in tightly covered containers. Substitute anise extract, but use it very sparingly.

花 椒

SZECHWAN PEPPER (FAGARA): Speckled brown peppercorns with a mildly hot flavor and a pleasant scent. Sold whole, not ground, by weight in Chinese specialty shops. It will keep indefinitely in tightly covered containers. No substitute.

西 米 粉

TAPIOCA FLOUR: Waxy-textured flour made from the same cassava root that is the basis of tapioca. Sold in 1-pound plastic bags in Oriental and health-food shops. Store as you would regular wheat flour. No substitute.

皮 蛋

THOUSAND-YEAR EGGS: Duck eggs that have been coated with a paste of ashes, lime and salt, and buried for two months. Sold individually in Chinese specialty stores. Will keep for about a month. No substitute.

金 針

TIGER LILY BUDS, DRIED: Pale-gold lily buds about 2 to 3 inches long. Sold by weight in Chinese specialty shops. Store in a covered container. No substitute.

麵 筋

VEGETABLE STEAK: A vegetarian food that looks like a small beefsteak but is made from wheat gluten. Sold in cans in Oriental and health-food stores. No substitute.

馬蹄

WATER CHESTNUTS: Walnut-sized
bulbs with tough, brown skins and
crisp, white meat. Sold fresh by
weight in Chinese specialty shops
and in various-sized cans whole,
sliced or diced, in supermarkets as
well. Store fresh ones refrigerated
for several days. After opening
canned ones, drain and refrigerate in
water in a covered jar for about a
month, changing the water daily.
No substitute.

澄粉

WHEAT STARCH: Wheat flour with
the gluten extracted. Sold in 1-
pound sacks in Chinese specialty
shops. Store like regular flour. No
substitute.

冬瓜

WINTER MELON: Round, green-
skinned melons of varying sizes. The
pulp is translucent and white. Its
flavor most resembles that of
zucchini or other soft-skinned
squash. Sold fresh in slices by weight
in Chinese specialty stores. Keep in
refrigerator for 3 to 5 days with cut
surfaces covered with plastic wrap.
Substitute zucchini or cucumber.

How to Use Chinese Recipes

When a hostess begins planning a menu based on one of the traditional Western cuisines, she may have a few problems arising out of seasonal availability of certain ingredients. But, generally speaking, she is on familiar ground, and she can proceed confidently in her choice of appetizer, soup, entrée, vegetables, salad and dessert. Chinese meals are a special problem because the categories are different.

In the first place, a Chinese meal is rather like a buffet, at which a guest eats little bits of this and that rather than a large portion of just one food. Chinese dishes are not served in individual portions, but are platters shared by all those who sit at the table. Everyone can—indeed he is expected to—eat from all the dishes presented.

A properly planned dinner includes at least one fowl, one fish and one meat dish—and these are complemented with appropriate vegetables. The Chinese set off spicy dishes with bland ones, delicate flavors with robust; and soft-textured foods are complemented by something crisp.

Concerned as they are with the appearance of food, the Chinese try to include both pale and richly colored dishes, and make a point of serving some bright-green vegetables for contrast.

While the Chinese serve many dishes at a meal, they do not—except at elaborate banquet-style dinners—present a menu in courses. Cold foods, meant to be nibbled like hors d'oeuvre, are sometimes placed on the table before the guests are seated. Otherwise, all the dishes are brought to the table at one time and eaten together. Hot tidbits like shrimp toast are classic banquet fare, brought to the table throughout the meal.

Although they are famous for excellent soups, the Chinese serve them in what may seem surprising ways. In some cases, soups appear early in the meal, but the light broths might be sipped throughout, and both the broths and richer, cornstarch-thickened soups like velvet corn or sour-and-hot soup may be presented separately in the middle of a dinner. The heavy, full-meal soups like *wonton* and Chinese noodle soup are most often eaten as lunches or snacks, though sometimes they become a part of the menu for a special occasion such as a birthday banquet.

You will find a number of so-called salads in this book, but the Chinese do not have a word for salad in the familiar sense of raw greens tossed with dressing. In China uncooked vegetables rarely appear at the table. Cold cooked vegetable dishes, dressed with soy sauce, wine and seasonings—and equivalent to the Western salad in many ways—are sometimes part of the main meal, but they also may be part of a cold hors d'oeuvre plate.

Desserts as such are practically unknown in China, though some hosts serve fresh fruit after a meal. Sweets included in this book would usually be served between courses at a Chinese banquet.

Since a full meal requires such a careful balance of foods—and the preparation of many new dishes at once—it may be easiest to start out by using the recipes in this book for simple substitutions in Western-style meals. A Chinese vegetable might be sampled one day, a chicken dish the next, while you stick to the sequence of courses you are used to. In this way you can perfect Chinese cooking techniques one at a time and gradually get acquainted with the special tastes of Chinese foods and seasonings.

In many cases, one Chinese preparation can replace several Western ones, for among their dishes are numerous combinations of meat or seafood and vegetables—equivalents to our stews and casseroles. One authority distinguishes between the "light meat dishes," which are more vegetable than meat, and the "heavy meat dishes," in which the proportions are reversed. If you plan to serve chicken with bean sprouts, bear in mind that it will take the place of both a chicken and a vegetable dish in your menu.

The number of guests that a dish will serve depends on whether you are planning it as part of a Western meal or using it in a fully Chinese menu. The Western-style helpings would probably be larger and the dish would serve fewer guests than it might in a Chinese dinner.

The number of dishes you can serve easily is also influenced by the way they must be cooked. One of the most frequently used of Chinese techniques is the stir-fry method—constant lifting and turning of small pieces of food to cook them quickly. This is simple enough to master, but stir-fried dishes, like other short-order foods, are meant to be brought to the table the minute they are done and served piping hot. And only one pound of meat can be stir-fried at one time. In all likelihood, one modest stir-fried dish per meal will be all you can handle at first.

After a few successful experiments with several different recipes, your understanding of Chinese methods will have grown sufficiently so that you are ready to undertake a full Chinese meal. The easiest way to do this is to plan to serve only two or three Chinese dishes—maybe a soup and two main courses—together with the traditional rice and tea, and fresh fruit for dessert. If the quantities in a recipe seem small, you may double them; but when you double a stir-fry recipe, you must make it in two batches using separate woks or skillets.

With a little practice, you will quickly gain the confidence to try full-scale dinners. In your menus, combine foods that are stir-fried or deep-fried, thus requiring last-minute attention, with others than can be finished earlier and kept warm in their pots. Try to mix a variety of basic foods (meat, poultry, fish or seafood), of tastes, of textures, of colors, in typical Chinese style. You may conclude with dessert if you wish, but you will prove yourself an old China hand by omitting it.

Drawings by Matt Greene, photographs by Charles Phillips.